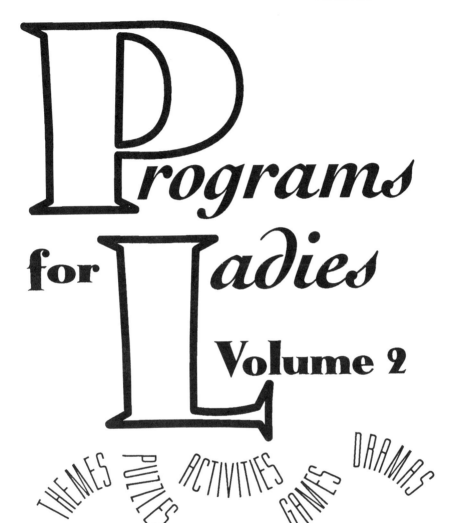

Programs for Ladies

Volume 2

THEMES PUZZLES ACTIVITIES GAMES DRAMAS

For Ladies' Meetings, large or small, Banquets, Retreats, Conventions, Showers, Special Services

by Barbara Westberg

Programs for Ladies
Volume II

Barbara Westberg

©1993 Word Aflame Press
Hazelwood, MO 63042-2299

Cover Design by Tim Agnew

Printed in United States of America

Printed by

Library of Congress Cataloging-in-Publication Data
(Revised for vol. 2)

Westberg, Barbara.
    Programs for ladies.

    Includes bibliographical references and indexes.
    Contents: [v. 1] Themes and complete programs for banquets & retreats, adaptable for special services, auxiliary meetings, and conventions — v. 2. Themes, dramas, games, puzzles, activities for ladies' meetings, large or small, banquets, retreats, conventions, showers, special services.
    1. Women, Pentecostal—Societies and clubs. 2. Holidays—Exercises, recitations, etc. 3. Pentecostal churches:—United States—Membership. I. Title.

BX8762.Z5W47 1990   246'.7   89-49113
ISBN 0-932581-61-7 (v. 1)
ISBN 1-56722-010-X (v. 2)

Contents

Acknowledgments 5
A Word about Skits 7

BANQUET THEMES
  1. A Flower Show 11
  2. As It Was in the Days of 17
  3. Hand-Me-Down Faith 33
  4. Mothers in Israel 41
  5. Mothers Memorial 47
  6. Music Notes 61
  7. Reflections 67
  8. The Land of Make Believe 75
  9. The Quilting Bee 81
 10. Wash Day 87

DRAMAS
Synopses of Dramas 97
  1. A Goodly Heritage 99
    Scene I: The Glory of the Past
    Scene II: The Glory of Suffering
    Scene III: To God Be the Glory
    Scene IV: Beholding the Glory

  2. A Role Play 131
    Scene I: Let's Play Like
    Scene II: In Real Life
    Scene III: The Last Act

  3. School Days 159
    Scene I: My Load's Heavier Than Yours
    Scene II: Comfort Ye, My People
    Scene III: A Look in the Backpacks
    Scene IV: My Burden Is Light

  4. The Race 183
    Scene I: The CROSSroads (The Past)
    Scene II: The Road Ahead (The Future)
    Scene III: EnJOYing the Trip (The Present)

Index 205

Acknowledgments

A big thank you to my mother, Marcella Coffman, for the many hours she spent proofreading my manuscripts. As a mother and a proofreader, she's tops.

Another oversized thank you to Margie McNall who struggled with capitals, italics, indentions and all the other nitty-gritty bits of layout. She suggested the first *Programs for Ladies* and has cheered me on through both volumes.

A Word about Skits

Skits can be valuable vehicles for conveying important messages that might not reach their destination by other means. But if they are not closely monitored, skits can get out of control and run roughshod over folks.

In planning and producing skits, remember the rules covering humor:

1. Keep it kind.
2. Keep it clean.

What would be a fun-filled, exciting ride to one group may be a horrifying, degrading trip to another. For example: if someone in the audience has recently had brain surgery (or someone in her family has brain cancer or Alzheimer's), the skit "Mrs. Skinflint's Surgery" (normally hilarious) could be offensive to them. Most elderly people enjoy a good skit about forgetfulness, poor vision or hearing, etc.—if the characters are funny and lovable, not stupid and vulgar. Obesity, stuttering, mental retardation, along with many other disabilities, are touchy subjects. Before choosing a skit, take a mental overview of the audience.

In this book, I have attempted to write skits that do more than take you on a merry-go-round of laughs. They are designed to carry the audience on a funny, clean, kind ride that takes them somewhere.

I hope you enjoy the trip.

Banquet Themes

1

A Flower Show

Consider the lilies of the field, how they grow; they toil not, neither do they spin: And yet I say unto you, That even Solomon in all his glory was not arrayed like one of these (Matthew 6:28-29).

DECORATIONS: To spread the work around and add a creative touch to your banquet, encourage the ladies to enter your "Flower Show." Flowers must be home grown or wild. To assure that you have enough arrangements for centerpieces, announce that ladies should sign up at least one week in advance to be eligible for prizes. Announce the details of the contest before the banquet and include them in all posters and invitations.

Ask guests who have not entered the contest to serve as judges. Unusual vases picked up at garage sales or second-hand stores could be the prizes.

SONGS: "Little Flowers," "Every Prayer Is a Flower"

PUZZLE

(Print this puzzle on the program for a prebanquet activity.)

Say It with Flowers

Fill in the blanks with the names of flowers, one letter per blank.

1. _ _ _/_ _ _ _ _ _ _ leave one laughing? You will think

so by the time you finish this quiz.

2. Did the __ __ __/__ __ __ __ in the mud in the barn lot?

3. Leo is a __ __ __ __ __/__ __ __ __.

4. Let's wrap up in a blanket, sit in the window seat and watch the __ __ __ __/__ __ __ __ gently on the ground.

5. "Your __ __/__ __ __ __ are like a strand of scarlet," Solomon told his beloved.

6. "He can __ __/__ __ __ a trooper," said the old man.

7. "Silence is __ __ __ __ __ __ __," __ __ __ Sterling said.

8. "Will you get the __ __ __ __ __ __/__ __ __ out of the refrigerator?" Mother asked. "We need it for our bread."

9. I __ __/__ __ __ the name of her boyfriend, and she replied, "__ __ __ __ __/__ __ __ __ __ __ __."

10. "Wait," the mother warned her teenage daughter. "__ __-__ __ __ __ __ __ will get you in trouble."

11. "__ __/__ __ __/__ __, rascal," the hillbilly ordered. "Your __ __ __ __ __ needs you to plow in the field."

12. What a beautiful __ __ __ __ __ __ __. __ __ __ __ __ to God.

13. Why did __ __ __ __ __/__ __ __ __ her C.D. player? Was it to pay her electric bill?

14. "The whole show is just a __ __ __ __," __ __ __ __ __ Hudson declared.

15. In America everyone has an automobile. You could say this is a __ __ __/__ __ __ __ __ __.

16. "Oh, I just love to see my __ __ __ __/__ __ __/__ __ __ __/__ __ __-__ __ __," gushed the preacher's bride.

17. "Where did you get the recipe for this __ __ __ __ __/__ __ __ salad?"

18. The class dismisses promptly at __ __ __ __/__'__ __ __ __ __.

[ANSWERS: 1. May/flowers 2. cow/slip 3. dande/lion 4. snow/drop 5. tu/lips 6. li/lac 7. golden/rod 8. butter/cup 9. as/ter, sweet/william 10. impatiens 11. be/gon/ia, poppy 12. morning/glory 13. holly/hock 14. sham/rock 15. car/nation 16. jack/in/the/pulpit 17. sweet/pea 18. four/o'clock]

ACTIVITY

Giving Roses Now

When Anne of Green Gables was reprimanded for making so many mistakes, she replied, "But just think of all the mistakes I could have made, but didn't."

Do you get weary of reading about all the mistakes parents have made and are making? In this activity we will zero in on what mothers did right.

Give each person a pencil and a sheet of colored note paper, shaped like a rose. Ask her to write down one major thing her mother did right and the impact it had upon her life. Allow time for each lady to share her thoughts. Precious memories will be made as daughters share feelings they have never before expressed. Give (or mail) the notes to the mothers.

SKIT

Fretful Flowers

CAST: Lily, Daffodil, Tulip

PROPS: flower masks, large brown blanket, three chairs

INSTRUCTIONS: Make masks by sketching the flowers on colored posterboard, sized to cover a lady's face. Cut out the center of the masks for faces. Attach strings to sides.

Before guests arrive, place three chairs on one side of the platform and cover with a brown blanket. Place a portable microphone under the blanket. Most of the action and speaking takes place "underground." The flower talking should move around a lot so the audience can identify her. Daffodil sits in the middle.

To allow cast members time to slip under the brown blanket unnoticed, the Narrator leads the audience in an imaginary pantomime that requires them to keep their eyes closed.

NARRATOR: For a few seconds, we are going to pretend this room is a giant flower bed. Since we are all a little daffy, let's be daffodils. Just follow my instructions.

Close your eyes tightly, please.

(While eyes are closed and Narrator talks, the members of the cast, wearing their masks, slip into the room, sit in the chairs on the stage and hide under the brown blanket.)

It is cold and dark here underground. It has been winter for a long, long time. Brrrrrrrr. Shiver. Keep your eyes closed! Remember you are underground and can't see a thing.

Feel the damp earth surrounding you. But what is happening? It's getting warmer and warmer and warmer and warmer. In fact, it is so warm you feel like you must have some fresh air or you will burst.

So you straighten your back and push your stem up, up, up through the crust of the earth into the sunlight. Stand up. Your petals (eyes) open. And you bloom into a beautiful yellow daffodil, waving gently in the breeze.

Now turn to your neighbor and say, "You're daffy, but you're beautiful."

Thank you. You may be seated.

TULIP: *(stretches and stirs under cover)* Lily! Daffy! It's spring. Time to get up.

LILY: *(stirs and yawns loudly)* Not already! I just got to sleep.

DAFFODIL: *(curls up under blanket)* Snush the pooze button, Lily . . . I mean, push the snooze button. You know it always freezes at least once after the first thaw. If we head our sticks out now, I mean hick our steads out now, I mean stick our heads out now, Old Man Winter's sure to blow his icy breath town our dems, I mean, down our stems.

LILY: *(shivers)* I remember last year every time I tried to get up, some kid on a riding lawn mower cut me down. I don't know if it's even worth the effort to get out of bed.

TULIP: I know, Lily. The same thing happened to me. It's cozy and safe down here. Who knows what is waiting for us aboveground?

DAFFODIL: I know one thing, I'm yick of shellow.

LILY: Yick O'Shallow? Who's Yick O'Shallow?

DAFFODIL: I'm sick of yellow.

LILY: Ahhh, Daffy, yellow's not so bad. What if all you had was white?

DAFFODIL: White is very becoming on you, Lily, but I like variety. I've been thinking about dying my retals ped, I mean, my petals red.

TULIP: A red daffodil? Yuk!

DAFFODIL: I knew you wouldn't understand, Tulip. Your wardrobe is full of bright colors.

TULIP: It's true we tulips come in different colors, but I sure get tired of the same old style. How do you think I'd look styled like a poppy?

LILY: Like you'd gone to seed!

DAFFODIL: Oh, girls, go sack to beep, I mean, back to sleep.

FLOWERS curl up and snore for a few seconds.

DAFFODIL: *(wiggles and nudges others)* Move over, Lily. Tulip, you're crowding me.

LILY: We're crowding you? You're the one who's taking your half in the middle.

TULIP: It sure is getting stuffy in here.

LILY: It's warm, too.

DAFFODIL: And crowded! I said, move over!

LILY: If you want someone to move, you move!

TULIP: *(chokes)* No, don't, Daffy! Every time you move, I get a mouthful of dirt. I've got to have some fresh air. I've got to get out of here.

DAFFODIL: But do we dare show our faces? What about Old Man Winter?

LILY: *(peeks out from under blanket)* I don't know. It looks like the sun is shining, but you can't believe everything you see.

DAFFODIL: What about the kid on the mawn lower, I mean, the lawn mower?

LILY: I don't hear him, but you can't believe everything you hear, or don't hear, either.

TULIP: It's pretty comfortable here in our bed.

DAFFODIL: You mean, it *was* pretty comfortable. I'm getting cramped. I wish I had a different dolor cress, I mean, color dress, to wear.

TULIP: And I wish I had a different style.

LILY: I wish I had room to breathe. I'm getting up. *(pops out from under cover)*

DAFFODIL & TULIP: *(pop up together)* We are too.

FLOWERS takes great gulps of air.

TULIP: Wow! What a beautiful world!

LILY: Yeah, I'd stayed undercover for so long, I'd almost forgotten how nice it is in the sunshine.

DAFFODIL: And I'd forgotten how pretty yellow is. Imagine a daffodil any other color. Why, it would be dumb plaffy, I mean, plumb daffy.

TULIP: And imagine a tulip any other style.

LILY: It's a good thing spring made us get up. Much longer underground and we'd have rotted!

DAFFODIL: We were already tetting and frewing, I mean, fretting and stewing like humans. And that's about as faffy as dowers, I mean as daffy as flowers can get.

FLOWERS EXIT, running.

ADDITIONAL SKIT

"A Petunia in an Onion Patch" from the first volume of *Programs for Ladies,* page 11, also goes well with this theme.

2

As It Was in the Days of . . .

But as the days of Noe were, so shall also the coming of the Son of man be (Matthew 24:37).

DECORATIONS: From women who are going to be attending the banquet borrow Bibles that have special significance, such as an old family Bible, a bride's Bible, a child's Bible. Use these for centerpieces by placing them on stand-up plate or book holders. Add a bow or an attractive bookmark, and arrange silk greenery around the base.

The outstanding decor of this banquet will be the ladies themselves. Each one is to come dressed as a specific Bible woman. Ask them to not tell anyone whom they are going to be, as part of the program will be guessing each one's identity. To help others identify them, they can carry clues. For example, Hannah or Dorcas might carry a sewing basket, Mary a perfume bottle, Martha a broom or dust cloth. Encourage them to be creative and do their biblical homework.

If you plan to use one or more of the skits included in this program, the cast members will have preassigned identities for the drama. However, no one else should know their identity.

FAVORS: Give hand-made bookmarks, crocheted or handpainted.

PUZZLE: *(Copy this crossword puzzle onto the program for early birds to work while they wait for the banquet to begin. They may need to use the Bible centerpieces to find the answers.)*

The Bible mentions many different kinds of women. To work this crossword puzzle, fill in the blanks.

1. (down) "Yea, and _____ women also of our company made us astonished" (Luke 24:22).

2. (down) "And all the women that were _____ _____ did spin with their hands" (Exodus 35:25).

3. (down) "The _____ women likewise, that they be in behaviour as becometh holiness" (Titus 2:3).

4. (across) "The hands of the _____ women have sodden their own children" (Lamentations 4:10).

5. (down) "Consider ye, and call for the _____ women, that they may come" (Jeremiah 9:17).

6. (across) "But the Jews stirred up the _____ and honourable women" (Acts 13:50).

7. (across) "And some of them believed . . . and of the ____ women, not a few" (Acts 17:4).

7. (down) "Many days and years shall ye be troubled, ye _____ women" (Isaiah 32:10).

8. (down) "The _____ women as mothers . . ." (I Timothy 5:2).

9. (down) "And send for _____ women, that they may come" (Jeremiah 9:17).

10. (across) "Kings' daughters were among thy _____ women" (Psalm 45:9).

18

10. (down) "For after this manner in the old time the _____ women also, who trusted in God, adorned themselves" (I Peter 3:5).

11. (across) "There shall yet old men and _____ women dwell in the streets of Jerusalem" (Zechariah 8:4).

12. (across) "For of this sort are they which creep into houses, and lead captive _____ women laden with sins" (II Timothy 3:6).

ANSWERS

```
                              C
                              E
                              R
                              T
                      W       A
    A             P   I   T   I   F   U   L
    G     M       S           N
D   E V O U T     E               C   H   I   E   F
    D     U       H               A           L
          R   C   E               R           D
    H O   N O U   R   A   B   L   E           E
    O     I   N   R       O   L   D           R
    L     N   N   T               E
    Y     G   I   E               S
              N   D               S   I   L   L   Y
              G
```

SHARING TIME

The Story of My Bible

Ask the women whose Bibles are displayed to be prepared to briefly share the sentimental significance of that Bible to their family.

GAME

The Revealing
Who Am I?

On part of the printed program, leave a blank space for guests to guess the other ladies' biblical identities. They may be working on this as the ladies enter and during the meal.

Before the "revealing," allow a few minutes for each one to march across the podium. They could even give one verbal clue (not too easy) as to their identity.

For the revealing, ask each lady to stand and "introduce" herself. Give prizes to:

1. the one with the most original costume.
2. the one portraying the least known Bible character.
3. the one guessing the most identities.

SKIT

Nothing New under the Sun

ENTER REPORTER, dressed in modern clothes, carrying a pencil and a clipboard holding the script.

REPORTER: Wow! What luck! I've been assigned to interview women on issues relevant to our day. And here I find not just one lady but a group of ladies. I should be able to get all the material I need for my article at one stop.

What shall I cover first? *(Scans paper on clipboard.)* How about alcoholism? Alcohol is one of the leading chemical drugs of our day. Is anyone here married to an alcoholic? Are you willing to talk to me about it?

ABIGAIL stands.

ABIGAIL: I'll talk to you provided you promise not to use my name in your article because my present husband is very well known.

REPORTER: I will protect your identity.

ABIGAIL goes to stand beside the REPORTER. Reporter takes notes as she talks.

REPORTER: You mentioned your "present husband." How many times have you been married?

ABIGAIL: Two.

REPORTER: Is your present husband an alcoholic?

ABIGAIL: Oh, no. It was my first husband.

REPORTER: What kind of a man was he?

ABIGAIL: He was a rich man.

REPORTER: A rich man? Yet an alcoholic? Hummmm, that's a little contrary to the norm, isn't it? I thought most drunks were poor and ignorant.

ABIGAIL: Alcoholism touches all social and intellectual levels. My husband was rich and wicked. The servants called him "a son of Belial." He was a worthless, lawless, foolish man. When he was drinking, he was terribly cruel.

REPORTER: Ahhhh, yes, drunk men often are.

ABIGAIL: Once when he was drinking, he did something very stupid that could have cost him his life. Only because of my intervention was he spared.

REPORTER: Where is this man now?

ABIGAIL: He's dead. When he sobered up after pulling the stupid act that I mentioned, I told him what had happened. It shook him up so that he had a stroke. Ten days later he died.

REPORTER: Ahhhhhh, I believe I recognize you. Aren't you King Da—?

ABIGAIL: Sssshhhh! You promised not to reveal my identity. Just let me say this. Alcoholism is nothing new. It's been a problem since Noah planted a vineyard, made wine and got drunk. Sometimes the wife of an alcoholic feels like she is all alone and no one understands her problem. But the truth is, women for centuries have suffered as she is suffering.

REPORTER: Is that suppose to be comforting?

ABIGAIL: Strangely enough, it is. Shared pain is always lessened.

REPORTER: That's true. I guess it's just human nature to feel better if we know we're not the only ones going through the fire. Thank you, Mrs. Abig—

ABIGAIL: (*finger to lips*) Sssshhhh! You promised not to use my name.

ABIGAIL returns to her seat.

REPORTER: Well, let's move on to another subject. How about racial prejudice? Has anyone here ever suffered from racial prejudice?

ESTHER stands.

ESTHER: I have.

REPORTER: You? But you are a queen! How could you know anything about racial prejudice?

ESTHER moves to the front.

ESTHER: Because I look like everyone else in the kingdom—oh, maybe a little prettier than the average—no one can tell my race by looking at me.

REPORTER: What is your race?

ESTHER: I am a Jew.

REPORTER: A Jew? I'm beginning to understand. For some reason Jews have been the target of racial harrassment and prejudices for centuries. Tell us your experience.

ESTHER: When I was chosen as queen, no one in the palace knew I was a Jew. But when the wicked Haman started his campaign to destroy all the Jews, my cousin Mordecai told me that I had to reveal my true identity to the king and intercede for my people. He said perhaps that was the reason God had allowed me to become queen.

REPORTER: And so . . .

ESTHER: So I did what Mordecai asked, but not before calling all Jews to prayer and fasting.

REPORTER: Surely as queen you didn't have anything to fear.

ESTHER: Oh, but I did. You have to understand that King Ahasuerus was a very temperamental man. He had divorced Queen Vashti simply because she refused to obey one order. I didn't know when I walked into that throne room whether the king would shout, "Off with her head,'' or say lovingly, ''Whatever you want, dearest, it is yours.''

REPORTER: So what did happen?

ESTHER: I interceded for the Jews and God interceded for me. King Ahasuerus granted me my request and the Jews were spared.

REPORTER: What about the wicked Haman?

ESTHER: (shudders) Even that name is repulsive to me. If you think your generation has a monopoly on sexual harrassment, you should have lived in my day. Haman was a vulgar, dirty man. He was hanged on the gallows he had built for my cousin Mordecai. And Mordecai was given Haman's position in the kingdom. God always has a way of balancing the scales for His people.

REPORTER: Thank you, Queen Esther.

ESTHER returns to her seat.

REPORTER: So we see alcoholism, racial prejudices, and sexual harrassment are not confined to our generation. But what about homosexuality? It's an ugly subject, but one we hear about almost every day. Has the family of anyone here ever been crippled by this sin?

NOAH'S WIFE stands and moves to the front.

NOAH'S WIFE: Mine has. I had three sons: Ham, Shem and Japheth. God saved our family from the flood, and we thought were ''home safe.'' Although we didn't say so in so many words, we were beginning to believe in eternal security, at least for us.
    But after the flood, the seeds of sin that had been planted in Ham by the wicked preflood generation began to sprout. It was a sad day for our family when Ham's evil thoughts bore fruit. It broke our hearts to realize that out of the eight people saved in the ark, one of them had such a perverted mind and sinful nature.

REPORTER: What happened to Ham?

NOAH'S WIFE: God placed a curse on him, and our family was divided and scattered.

REPORTER: Tell me, Mrs. Noah, how did you cope with this?

NOAH'S WIFE: The only way I could, with tears and prayers. I grieved and I agonized. I coped with my pain as all mothers cope when one of their children goes astray. For months I just survived. Then one day I realized I could recall the good memories and smile. Eventually, I could even smile at the present.

REPORTER: Thank you, Mrs. Noah, for letting us look into the corners of your heart and see your pain. Maybe it will help other mothers with wayward children to realize they can survive, and even eventually smile again.

NOAH'S WIFE returns to her seat.

Let's move on and talk about another issue of our day, the cancer of our society which strikes millions of families every year—divorce. Who would be willing to talk to me about your divorce?

GOMER rises and comes to the front.

GOMER: It's not easy to talk about that time in my life, but I will if it will help someone else.

REPORTER: Thank you, Mrs.—?

GOMER: Mrs. Hosea. My first name is Gomer.

REPORTER: Tell me, Mrs. Hosea, what did your husband do to cause you to divorce him?

GOMER: I didn't divorce him. He divorced me. He was a good man, a very good man, a prophet of God.

REPORTER: So you were the preacher's wife? How could your husband divorce you?

GOMER: Oh, he had lots of grounds for divorce. You see, I left him and my three beautiful children for another man, a rich man.

REPORTER: But why?

GOMER: *(shrugs)* Who can explain the insanity of lust? Before I married, I had been wild. Everyone thought I had changed, but deep down inside I was the same old Gomer. Yes, Hosea had every right to divorce me. And knowing it was my fault didn't make it any easier.

REPORTER: Did you marry your rich lover?

GOMER: *(laughs harshly)* Marry him? Oh, no. He cast me off like chaff in the wind. I found myself back walking the streets and eventually on a slave's auction block.

REPORTER: How terrible! Then what happened?

GOMER: Hosea . . . Hosea happened to walk by that day as I was being sold into slavery. He bought me back. My husband redeemed me. How he could still love me, I didn't know. But he did.

REPORTER: I know it has hurt you to stir up these memories, Gomer. But let me ask you one more thing, what would you say to any woman going through a divorce?

GOMER: I would say to her, no matter what you have done or what has been done to you, God loves you. He paid the supreme price to redeem you. Don't cast away His love.

GOMER returns to her seat.

REPORTER: I have enough material here for several articles. Now, let me see, what is the common message of these interviews? Abiga . . . Oops! I almost said her name. I'll start over. What is the common message—from the lady who had an alcoholic husband, from a queen's experience with racial prejudice and sexual harrassment, from a mother's heartbreak over a wayward son, from an unfaithful wife reaping the seeds of lust and greed? The common message: there is nothing new under the sun. Whatever you are going through, ladies, women in generations before you, even back to Bible days, walked those same paths and survived. In fact, they did better than survive. They overcame. And you can, too!

Remember this: *"There hath no temptation taken you but such as is common to man: but God is faithful, who will not suffer you to be tempted above that ye are able; but will with the temptation also make a way to escape, that ye may be able to bear it"* (I Corinthians 10:13).

SKIT

A Mother-Daughter Tea

CAST: Sarah, Rebekah, Rachel, Asenath, Linda Jo

PROPS: table, 5 chairs, tea pot, tea cups and saucers, sugar, lemon, sweetener

INSTRUCTIONS: Table and four chairs set up for tea centerstage. An extra chair is sitting on one side.

NARRATOR: Somewhere in a unique little tea shop in the mall of eternity, four generations of ladies from Abraham's family meet for a chitchat.
    Let's eavesdrop. Quietly now. We don't want them to know we're within a hundred years.

ENTER BIBLE LADIES, take their places around the table.

SARAH: Ahhhhh, this is nice, having my girls around me. It's one advantage of being in eternity, no generation gaps.

RACHEL: I know, Grandmother Sarah. On earth I never even met my husband's mother, let alone his grandmother. You don't look nearly as old as I thought you would.

SARAH: Another advantage of eternity, Rachel my dear. One of the first things I shed when I arrived was wrinkles. What a face lift!

REBEKAH: Just walking through the door, I dropped fifty pounds. Talk about heaven!

RACHEL: I can hardly believe I am having tea with my grandmother-in-law, Sarah; my mother-in-law, Rebekah; and my daughter-in-law, Asenath.

ASENATH: Shall I pour? How do you like your tea, Grandmother Sarah?

SARAH: *(responds appropriately)* Thank you, my dear. Now let's see, which one of the boys did you marry?

ASENATH pours Sarah's tea.

REBEKAH: I'm surprised you can't remember, Mother Sarah.

SARAH: My dear Rebekah, there are some things even heaven can't correct. Besides you'll have to admit that Jacob had a whole tribe of boys. I doubt if you could name all your grandsons.

ASENATH: I was married to Joseph, Grandmother Sarah.

SARAH: Ahhhh, yes, Joseph. He was one of my favorites.

REBEKAH: But, Mother, you were dead long before Joseph was born.

SARAH: Ahhhh, that I was. Well, I mean, he would have been one of my favorites.

ASENATH: He was a prince of a man.

ENTER LINDA JO, hair awry, clothes thrown on. She slumps into extra chair. Other ladies seem not to notice her.

LINDA JO: *(breathlessly)* I just can't believe I made it. I really didn't think I would. *(takes deep breath; notices tea party)* I wonder what's going on over there.

SARAH: *(peers at Asenath)* Now let's see, you are that Egyptian girl he married, right?

ASENATH: Yes, ma'am.

REBEKAH: I'll take my tea *(tells Asenath how she wishes her tea)*.

LINDA JO: Oh, they're having tea. Imagine a tea party in heaven. I sure could use a cup of tea. My poor nerves are shot!

REBEKAH: When we were back on earth, confined by time, Mother Sarah, I thought about you a lot—especially when Isaac moved me into *your* tent as soon as we were married! Talk about a mamma's boy!

SARAH: Now, Rebekah, you can't fault me too much for spoiling him. Think how long I waited to be a mother. And remember, you spoiled Jacob.

LINDA JO: I wonder how long it's going to take me to recover from my time on earth. I feel as jumpy as a jack-in-a-box.

RACHEL: Did she ever spoil him! And having my sister Leah and I fussing and fighting over him all the time didn't do anything to shrink his ego.

REBEKAH: Well, Isaac and I had been married twenty years before I got pregnant. Isaac often tried to encourage me by saying, "Don't fret, Rebekah, remember how old my mother was when I was born!" Some encouragement!

ASENATH: How would you like your tea, Mother Rachel?

RACHEL: I'll take it *(gives instructions)*. Thank you, my dear.

ASENATH serves Rachel, then herself. LINDA JO gets up and approaches table.

LINDA JO: Ahhhh, pardon me, but I . . . I . . . could I. . . .

REBEKAH: Well, hello. I don't believe we've met. Could we help you?

LINDA JO: Pardon me, but I'd love to have a cup of tea. You see, I just arrived and my nerves are still a bit on edge. You can't imagine how stressful life on earth is these days.

ASENATH brings Linda Jo's chair to the table and makes room for her.

REBEKAH: I'm Rebekah, wife of Isaac. This is my mother-in-law, Sarah, wife of Abraham. This is my daughter-in-law, Rachel, wife of Jacob, and her daughter-in-law, Asenath, wife of Joseph.

LINDA JO: *(sits down)* Oh, I never dreamed I'd have tea with you ladies. I'm so honored.

SARAH: And what did you say your name is?

LINDA JO: Didn't I say? Dear me, I'm so flustered . . . My name is Linda Jo Jackson.

ASENATH: Sit right here, Linda Jo. How do you like your tea?

LINDA JO: *(responds appropriately)*

SARAH: You look like you have been running.

LINDA JO: Oh, I have. Life on earth is one rat race. It's run, run, run! The stress is almost unbearable. I'm sure it got me here ten years early. But, please, ladies, don't let me hinder your conversation. I'll just sit quietly and try to pull myself together. *(sighs heavily)*

SARAH: *(to Asenath)* You have beautiful manners, child. Judah did well when he married you.

REBEKAH: Not Judah, Mother, Joseph.

SARAH: That's what I meant. Joseph did well when he married you even if you are a Midianite.

RACHEL: She's an Egyptian, Grandmother.

SARAH: That's what I meant . . . even if you are an Egyptian. Hagar was an Egyptian, too, but you're not one bit like her.

LINDA JO: An Egyptian? Aren't you a Hebrew, Sarah? Imagine an Egyptian and Hebrew having tea together. They sure didn't do that on earth.

SARAH: We had our differences in my day, too. *(to Asenath)* I suppose you had a very soft life, married to the second-in-command in Egypt.

ASENATH: It was a wonderful life until . . . until . . . well . . . .

RACHEL: Until what?

ASENATH: Well, I hesitate to say this because I wouldn't want to hurt anyone's feelings.

RACHEL: I don't know any reason it would hurt my feelings. After all, Asenath, I died long before you married Joseph. Anyway, this is heaven. No hurt feelings here.

LINDA JO: No hurt feelings here? Amazing!

ASENATH: It's just that . . . well, can you imagine what it would be like to have seventy in-laws dumped in your lap overnight?

LINDA JO: Seventy? Horrors! I only had one mother-in-law and two sisters-in-law. That was enough . . . more than enough!

RACHEL: *(coldly)* Perhaps you should explain, Asenath, and remember, it's my family you are referring to.

ASENATH: Oh, dear. I knew it would hurt your feelings. But when I married Joseph, I didn't even know he had a family. For several years it was just Joseph and me and the boys. Then suddenly Joseph's family showed up and Joseph moved them all to Egypt . . . all seventy of them!

SARAH: I can see that would have been a surprise.

LINDA JO: Surprise? It must have been a 220-volt jolt!

ASENATH: It was upsetting. Oh, I loved Father Jacob and most of the others. But it taxed my nerves for a time adjusting to such a large family. I'll tell you, I was stressed out!

LINDA JO: Stressed out? You? Back in Bible days?

SARAH: Talking about stress, imagine a ninety-year-old with a colicky baby, a smart-aleck teenage stepson, and a uppity-up maid!

RACHEL: At least, you only had one stepson, Grandmother Sarah. I had ten. The atmosphere in our family was as tight as a miser's pocketbook.

LINDA JO: My! My! I thought . . .

SARAH: Relationships on earth were pretty stressful, weren't they?

REBEKAH: I'll say. My boys were twins, but they were opposites. Esau was so rowdy and rough. All he had to do was walk through the tent and I felt like I'd been in a sandstorm. Now, Jacob, bless his little heart, was so gentle and quiet.

LINDA JO: Uh-ho. Sounds to me like you were partial.

REBEKAH: I hardly think it's any of your business.

RACHEL: As much as I loved your son and my husband, Mother Rebekah, I have to admit that he was sneaky and underhanded at times. He met his match in my father, Laban. They kept me uptight all the time.

LINDA JO: Where's the clock? I've got to run. *(peers at wrist)* Oh, I forgot. You sounded so much like ladies on earth, I forgot I'm in eternity. *(stands up)* No time.

SARAH: *(stands up)* No age.

REBEKAH: *(stands up)* No fat. No quarreling.

RACHEL: *(stands up)* No jealousy. No cheating.

ASENATH: *(stands up)* No in-laws.

SARAH, REBEKAH, RACHEL: Asenath!

ASENATH: *(laughs)* Sorry, ladies. I just couldn't resist.

LINDA JO: And best of all, no stress!

EXIT ALL

ALTERNATE SKIT

The drama "Through the Looking Glass" from *Programs for Ladies*, volume 1, would correlate with this banquet theme. This play also emphasizes that there is nothing new under the sun. If the entire drama is too much for your program, any of the Bible characters parts could be slightly adapted and used.

3

Hand-Me-Down Faith

*I call to remembrance the unfeigned faith that is
in thee, which dwelt first in thy grandmother Lois, and
thy mother Eunice; and I am persuaded that in thee
also* (II Timothy 1:5).

DECORATIONS: Set up the banquet room with small tables for six
or eight, instead of the usual U-shaped head table arrangement. Use
solid-colored tablecloths with contrasting place mats and napkins.

Place greenery, candles, silk flower arrangements, etc. (from your
home or borrowed) around the room to give a festive air.

Create a Centerpiece

Announce beforehand for all ladies or girls to bring one item that
has been handed down to them. They are not to tell anyone what they
are bringing. Do not tell them what they will be doing with the items
they bring.

Before the meal is served, allow about ten minutes for the ladies
at each table to arrange a centerpiece for their table using the hand-
me-downs they brought.

Either appoint a committee of judges or allow everyone to vote
on the winning centerpiece. Award each lady at that table a small
second-hand prize, picture frame, unique dish, etc. purchased at a
garage sale.

DOOR PRIZES: Give second-hand door prizes from garage sales to
the following: (1) the one wearing the most hand-me-down articles,
(2) the one bringing the oldest hand-me-down item, (3) the one with
the oldest lineage of Pentecostal ancestors. In case of a tie, have a
drawing.

SONGS: "Faith of Our Fathers [Mothers]" "The Old-Time Religion"

QUIZ

(Print this quiz on the back of the program and use for a time filler as you wait for everyone to arrive.)

Three-Generation Bible Families

Fill in the missing names in these three-generation families. Answers include both men and women.

1. Sarah, _____, Rachel
2. _____, Eunice, _____
3. Jochebed, _____, Abihu
4. Bathsheba, _____, Rehoboam
5. Naomi, _____, Obed
6. _____, _____, Esau
7. _____, _____, Ephraim
8. Ahaz, _____, Manasseh
9. Hagar, _____, Nebajoth
10. Terah, _____, Ishmael

[ANSWERS: 1. Rebekah 2. Lois, Timothy 3. Aaron 4. Solomon 5. Ruth 6. Abraham, Isaac 7. Jacob (Israel), Joseph 8. Hezekiah 9. Ishmael 10. Abram (Abraham)]

GETTING ACQUAINTED

Allow a few minutes for each lady to introduce herself and tell a little about the hand-me-down item she brought.

MONOLOGUE

Hand-Me-Down Faith

CAST AND PROPS: For GIRL—hair bow, teddy bear; for MOTHER —apron, dust cloth, and furniture polish; for GRANDMOTHER— shawl, Bible, glasses

INSTRUCTIONS: In this three-part monologue the same person portrays the three stages of a woman's life. Between each scene there is a special song, which allows time for the performer to catch her and change props.

Part I: Little Girl

ENTER LITTLE GIRL, wearing bow in hair, carrying teddy bear, sniffing.

It was just a little lie, a teeny-weeny little lie, not big enough for a spankin'. And it really wasn't even a lie . . . just a fib. I said I picked up my toys and I did. I picked 'em up and threw 'em under the bed.

And do you know what Mommy said, Teddy? Do you know what she said when she spanked me? She said, "This hurts me more than it hurts you." Bah! If it hurts her so bad, why does she do it? When I get to be a mommy, I'm never going to spank my little girl.

Why did I have to get the meanest mother in the whole wide world? Missie's mom never spanks her. She said spankings stifle creativity. What's creativity, Teddy? You don't know either? Whatever it is, *(wails)* mine's been stifled.

(Sniffs and wipes nose with back of hand) I know what I'm gonna do. I'm gonna run away. You'll go with me, won't you, Teddy? We'll run away and live with Grandma. Grandma will let me eat chocolate cake before dinner and stay up half the night and she never spanks me and . . . That's what we'll do, we'll run away. *(starts to leave)* I know the way to Grandma's house. She lives in the next block and . . . *(stops and turns around)* I just remembered. Mommy won't let me cross the street by myself. And she said you don't count, Teddy.

(Sits down) Now what are we going to do? We can't run away, and we can't stay here. Mommy's too mean.

(Looks up) Huh? Who was that? Did somebody call me? Is that You, Lord? It is! Ohhhh? I know you talk to Mommy all the time, but this is the first time You ever talked to me.

What? What did You say? Uhhhhh . . . uhhhhhh, what was I talking about? Oh . . . oh, me and Teddy we's just talking about Mommy. She's a . . . a good mommy. Yeah, Lord, she's really a good mommy.

What? Oh, she's been talking to You? Yeah, I know she talks to You every day. She thinks You can do anything . . . see in the dark, read lips, make good girls out of bad ones.

Oooohhh, she's been talking to You about me? Now, Lord, You know my mommy. She kinda . . . kinda ahhhhhh . . . oh, You know. She kinda 'zaggerates. Even little teeny-weeny fibs look like great big lies to her. Why she acts like a little bitty mouse is a dragon. You know, Lord, she's not as scared of the devil as she is a mouse.

Oh, You say we're getting off the subject? You say she talked to You about me this morning? Yeah, I know . . . uhhhhhh, she likes to talk. Just don't pay any 'tention to her. Daddy doesn't.

Would I like to know what she said? Ahhhhh, no, not really. . . . I'd be surprised? Yeah? But, Lord, You know all surprises aren't funny. . . . She said what? . . . My mommy said that? She told You that about me? You're sure You didn't get your calls mixed up? You're sure it was my mommy? And she said—she thanked You for giving me to her? She said I was precious? And she wanted more than anything to be a good mother?

Why, Lord, You know I wouldn't trade my mommy for Missie's mommy or any other mommy in the whole world, not even my grand-mommy.

(Listens) Oh, Teddy, that's Mommy callin' us now. Bet she wants me to pick up my toys again. When I get to be a mommy, I'll never make my little girl pick up her toys. I'll always . . . Oh, bye, Lord. And say, next time Mommy talks to You, would You tell her that all good mommies pick up their little girls' toys? She'll listen to You.

SONG: "Sunrise, Sunset"

Part II: Mother

ENTER MOTHER, wearing an apron, carrying a dust cloth and furniture polish.

Where does the time go? Seems like just yesterday I was a little girl, and now I've got two little girls and a husband and a house and two dogs and three kittens. Would you believe, my girls wanted me to buy them a white mouse? *(shudders)* I'm just like my mother, I'd have a dragon in this house before I'd have a mouse.

Man's work is from sun to sun, but woman's work is never done. I get the house cleaned and it's dirty again. Girls! Girls! Girls, go pick up your toys. Will they ever learn? I can't spend all my time picking up toys.

Training children is a lot more than telling them. It's telling them and telling them and telling them and . . . Girls, go pick up your toys right now!

(Sighs) Oh, Lord, You know that I want to be a good mother. I hate to nag. I really do. More than anything else in the world, I want to be a good mother. But I'm so confused. That magazine article I read the other day said, "Only tell a child to do a job one time." I

wonder what you're supposed to do then? Do the job, I guess. It also said, "Never spank a child when you're angry." If I don't spank them when I'm angry, I don't spank them. What mother spanks a child when she's happy? But it sure does hurt. It hurts me more than it does them. *(laughs)* I remember when I was a little girl, I declared I would never spank my children. Well, you live and learn.

Lord, please help me. You can make good mothers out of poor ones. Thank You for my children. They are a precious treasure.

(Dusts and sighs) My mother says I'm too uptight about this. That I should relax and enjoy them. She says I should trust You more, and I do trust You, Lord. You know I do. But I figure You trust me, too. You've trusted me with my children, but I've got to do it right the first time. This is not a practice run. It's the real thing.

Mother says no one ever died of gangrene from wearing dirty socks. She says I'm like an old mother hen clucking, cluck-cluck-clucking and gathering her chicks under her wings every time a cloud covers the sun.

Lord, would You do me a favor? Just give me strength for today. I'll talk to You again tomorrow, probably sooner. Now I've got to go help the girls pick up their toys.

EXITS

SONG: "One Day at a Time"

Part III: Grandmother

ENTER GRANDMOTHER, wearing shawl, glasses on nose, reading Bible.

"I have been young, and now I am old, but I have never seen the righteous forsaken; nor his seed begging for bread."

How the years have flown by. Here I am a little, well, maybe not too little, but an old lady. Know when I realized I was getting old? When I sat down in my rocking chair and couldn't get it started.

My, my, what changes I have seen! I remember when we bought ice cream cones at Glencliff's for five cents a dip. For a nickel you could buy a Grapette or mail a letter and two postcards. Or, you could make a phone call—if you could find a phone and a nickel at the same time. And if you knew someone with a phone to call.

In my day the day care center was the home. Child psychology was lining the kids up and using a peach tree limb. A dysfunction was a "nose out of joint." An egotist was someone "too big for his breeches." We knew how to take care of both in a few minutes. Never heard of counseling. Had lots of heart-to-heart talks, though.

I grew up when we had to empty the drip pan under the icebox—when everyone dressed in front of the fire on winter mornings—when one of the kids sat on top of the ice cream freezer while Daddy turned the crank.

How the years have flown. Now I'm Grandma . . . that's a nice word. I'd rather be a grandmother than a mother any day. My little granddaughter told her mother the other day that she liked to go to Grandma and Grandpa's house because they never say, "Pick up your toys," and there are always popsicles in the refrigerator.

Lord, You have been good to me. I had a good mother. She taught me responsibility and self-control. I thought she was the meanest mother in the whole world, until I had two little girls. Then I became the meanest mother in the whole world.

Nothing will teach a woman to pray like children. I learned to pray on my knees, on my back, on my feet—in bed, in the bathtub, in the car.

Dad and I thought those teens years were going to last forever, but they didn't. When the girls cut the apron strings, I almost hemorrhaged to death. Funny now . . . but it sure wasn't then.

But through it all, Lord, I've learned to trust You. The faith my mother handed down to me when I was just a little girl . . . the knowledge that You can do anything . . . see in the dark, read lips, make good mothers out of little girls . . . that faith has kept me going when the sign said, "Dead end."

Hand-me-down faith. The most valuable thing my mother ever gave me.

EXIT

SONG: "'Tis So Sweet to Trust in Jesus"

SPEECH OUTLINE

Contend for the Faith

I found it necessary and was impelled to write you and urgently appeal to and exhort you to contend for the faith which was once for all handed down to the saints—the faith which is that sum of Christian belief . . . which was delivered verbally to the holy people of God (Jude 3, *Amplified Bible*).

I. Handed-Down Faith (II Timothy 1:5)
   A. Second-hand clothes
   B. Hand-me-downs in two categories
      1. Junk
      2. Antiques
   C. Age of Nostaglia
      1. Search for roots in mobile society
      2. If it's not old, make it look that way!

II. Faith of our Mothers
   A. Timothy's Heritage (II Timothy 1:5)
   B. Our Pentecostal Heritage
      1. Hand-me-downs either appreciate or depreciate.
      2. For our faith to appreciate we must appreciate it.
   C. Hocking our Heirlooms
      1. II Chronicles 12:1-2, 9-10, 14
      2. In 1974 one out of twenty-four changed from their family's faith. In 1990 one out of three changed.

III. Contending for the Faith
   A. Fight the good fight (II Timothy 4:7)
   B. Refuse to hock your shield of faith (Ephesians 6:16)

4

Mothers in Israel

[There] arose a mother in Israel (Judges 5:7).

DECORATIONS: This theme demands elegance, crystal, and linen. If necessary, borrow crystal bowls and candelabras.

Fill each bowl with water and place in it a large single flower, such as a magnolia or whatever is in bloom.

In the center of each table set a bowl on a mirror tile.

Use white linen tablecloths and napkins.

Place crystal candelabras with white candles around the room.

QUIZ

(Put this quiz on the program for a prebanquet time filler.)

Whose Mother Said?

Fill in the blanks with a biblical mother who could have said the following.

1. "I was so proud of him. I never dreamed he'd become a jailbird. And all because of some mystical experience. Surely he's not on drugs." _____

2. "What? Not another fight! I told your dad a long time ago that you're too hot headed to carry a sword." _____

3. "Oh, no, not another daughter-in-law! Son, don't you realize this makes six hundred and thirteen?" _____

4. "I don't know how these boys can be twins and still be so different." _____

5. "Don't you get high-hat with me, young man, just because

you live in a palace. Remember, I'm your mother.'' _____
_____

6. "You're moving and not leaving a forwarding address? Son, you can't spend your life on a camping trip." _____
_____

7. "One of these days you're going to fall out of a tree and break your neck." _____

8. "You're pregnant? I can't believe it. You were always such a good girl." _____

9. "That's a whale of a story, but you're going to have to come up with a better one to account for your absence." _____
_____

10. "What's this red cord doing in the window? It doesn't even match the decor of this room." _____

11. "You mean you love your mother-in-law more than you do your own mother?" _____

12. "Go ahead and cross the river but don't get your feet muddy." _____

13. "What happened to your hair?" _____

14. "I told him not to wear his good coat for every day." __
_____

15. "He always has loved animals, but this is the limit." ____
_____

Now just for fun, think of another biblical character and write what his or her mother might have said. There will be time later in the program to let others guess the source of your quote.

_____
_____
_____
_____

[ANSWERS: 1. Paul's mother 2. Peter's mother 3. Bathsheba (Solomon's mother) 4. Rebekah (Jacob and Esau's mother) 5. Moses' mother 6. Abraham's mother 7. Zaccheus's mother 8. Mary's mother 9. Jonah's mother 10. Rahab's mother 11. Ruth's mother 12. Joshua's mother 13. Samson's mother 14. Joseph's mother (or possibly, Hannah, Samuel's mother) 15. Noah's mother]

ACTIVITY

My Mother Said

Ask three or four ladies to be prepared to share the wisest advice their mother ever gave them, and another three or four to share the funniest.

SKIT

Mothers in Israel

CAST: King's Herald, 2 King's Pages

PROPS: velvet capes for herald and pages, megaphone, scroll containing the royal decree, plaques or awards for mothers honored

ENTER KING'S PAGES, followed by the HERALD. The Herald carries a megaphone and the scroll.

HERALD: *(cries through megaphone)* Hear ye! Hear ye! All ye inhabitants of the land listen to the words of the King. Hear ye! Hear ye! The King has issued a royal decree ordering a search be made throughout the land for mothers.

PAGE I: Wait! Wait! You're looking for mothers?

HERALD: Yes. This royal decree reads, "A search shall hereby be made throughout the land for mothers."

PAGE I: Well, you've certainly come to the right place. Look around you.

HERALD: *(looks around)* So?

PAGE I: See any dads?

HERALD: No. *(If any are present, adapt the script accordingly.)*

PAGE I: See any mothers?

HERALD: Oh, just #___.*

PAGE I: So the search is over. You've found mothers.

PAGE II: What does the King want with mothers?

43

HERALD: That's the rest of the decree. If you will quit interrupting me, I'll finish. *(cries)* Hear ye! Hear ye! All ye inhabitants of the land listen to the words of the King. Hear ye! Hear ye!

PAGE II: I hear ye!

HERALD: Not me! Hear the King's royal decree. *(reads)* A search shall be made throughout the land of Israel for mothers. Godly mothers whose silent strength has undergirded the Old Ship of Zion when the winds of controversy threatened to shatter her . . . Christians mothers whose convictions have stood firm when morals all around were crumbling . . . Mothers who have been faithful, consistent, and dedicated.

PAGE I: That's a pretty big order, but I imagine there are at least #___** mothers here who fill that bill.

PAGE II: So the King sent you to find mothers in Israel? Here they are. Why has He issued a call for them?

HERALD: The King wishes us to give honor to whom honor is due.

PAGE II: So we are to give honor to #___** mothers?

PAGE I: That'll take all day, and we only have thirty minutes.

PAGE II: Correction. We only have twenty-six minutes left.

PAGE I: So what do we do?

HERALD: Relax. It's all in the program. Since it is impossible to give honor to every mother in Israel, we have chosen #___*** to represent the others. Now listen closely to your instructions. As I announce the names of the mothers in Israel we wish to honor, your job is to escort these lovely ladies to the platform. Think you can do that without tripping over your feet?

PAGES: We'll try.

HERALD takes place in center of stage with microphone.

FANFARE.

44

The HERALD announces the first name, using a few adjectives to describe the mother, such as "gentle and cheerful."

PAGES find the lady and escort her to the platform where she is seated.

FANFARE is repeated. The next name is called and the mother escorted to the platform. Continue until all to be honored are in place.

Suggestions for the remainder of the program:

1. A special song, such as "A Prayer Warrior," dedicated to these ladies.
2. Remarks by the pastor's wife.
3. A short introduction of each lady, followed by a "brief" testimony from the mother.
4. Presentation of plaques or awards.

* Approximate number of mothers present.
** Approximate number of Christian mothers who meet the requirements for being "a mother in Israel."
*** Number chosen to be honored.

5

Mothers Memorial

DECORATIONS: Use decorative jars filled with M & M's for center-pieces. Wrap a wide velvet ribbon around each jar and make a bow on the top. Use a red, green, and yellow color scheme.

From posterboard cut two large M's. Paint M & M's on them. Post on the wall in a prominent place.

FAVORS: Place a Mothers Memorial brochure (available from the Ladies Auxiliary of the United Pentecostal Church) and a small package of M & M's beside each place setting.

PUZZLE

Acronyms

(Print acronym puzzle from page 48 on the program for early birds to work while waiting for the banquet to begin.)

These familiar acronyms are part of our daily lives. But do you know what the initials stand for? Beneath each acronym write its meaning.

[ANSWERS: MM—Mothers Memorial; PK—preacher's kid; MYOB—mind your own business; AARP—American Association of Retired Persons; AIM—associate in missions; CFC—Christmas for Christ; PIM—partner-in-missions; UPCI—United Pentecostal Church International; IRS—Internal Revenue Service; NASA—National Aeronautics and Space Administration; YMCA—Young Men's Christian Association; WW—Weight Watchers; cc—carbon copy; SFC—Sheaves for Christ; HUD—Housing and Urban Development; ERA—Equal Rights Amendment; RSVP—Respondez, S'il Vous Plait (Respond, If You Please); FICA—Federal Insurance Contributions Act; SS—Social Security or Sunday School; PG—Parental Guidance or pregnant]

MM PK MYOB AARP AIM

CFC PIM UPCI IRS NASA

YMCA DD CC SFC HUD

ERA RSVP FICA SS PG

ACTIVITY

Mothers Memorial Is . . .

As each guest arrives give her a card divided into twenty-five squares (5 x 5) as in bingo. Mark the center square "free."

Instructions should be written at the top of the page.

From your Mothers Memorial brochure list twenty-four key words or phrases on your card (one item per box). Items listed could include: Tupelo Children's Mansion, dryer, dentist (or dental care), birthdays, foreign Bible school, etc.

To play, the leader reads paragraphs from the brochure, skipping around. Anytime a word or phrase is read that is on a player's card, the player places an "M & M" on that square (as in bingo). When a straight line has been formed, that player calls out, "Mothers Memorial." First player to completely fill her card is awarded one of the centerpieces.

SKIT

The First Ladies Auxiliary Project

CAST: Noah, Mrs. Noah

PROPS: miscellaneous carpenter tools, broom, clip board

SONG: "Noah Found Grace in the Eyes of the Lord" (verses 1 and 2)

NOAH ENTERS and pantomimes working as song is sung.

EXITS.

ENTER MRS. NOAH, carrying broom, wearing apron. Her hair is wrapped in a scarf.

MRS: Noah! Noah! Now where is that man? He's never home when I need the trash carried out. Probably gone on visitation again. I declare I would have given up long ago, but he keeps preaching to those sinners. Sometimes it seems like we're the only ones in the whole world trying to live right. I wish we could take a vacation and get away from all the wickedness around us. Wouldn't it be like heaven to take a cruise? But that's daydreaming. I might as well—

ENTER NOAH, whistling.

MRS: Oh, there you are. Have you been on outreach again? You know, Noah, no one is going to listen to you. Why don't we just take a vacation and forget about—

NOAH: No, I've not been on visitation. I've been talking to the Lord. Rather, He's been talking to me.

MRS: That's nice. Noah, I've been thinking. Let's take a vacation. I'd love to take a cruise. Remember when we got married, you promised—

NOAH: Well, now, honey, I just might be able to arrange that.

MRS: When we got married you promised—You what?

NOAH: I just might be able to arrange that!

MRS: I can't believe my ears. Oh, Noah, that would be wonderful! I never dreamed you'd say yes.

NOAH: Actually, a cruise fits right into my plans. You see, the Lord told me to build an ark.

MRS: An ark? What in the world is an ark?

NOAH: It's the vehicle that God is going to use to save this world.

MRS: Vehicle? You're going to build a vehicle? Now, Noah . . .

NOAH: Actually, it's a boat.

MRS: A boat? Noah, you're kidding me again.

NOAH: Not this time, honey.

MRS: You can't build a boat. You can't even build a storage shed. I've been after you for two years to build one.

NOAH: The Lord told me to build an ark, so I'm going to build an ark.

MRS: And what are you going to do with an ark of a boat out here in the middle of the plains?

NOAH: Ride in it when the flood comes. You want to go on a cruise, don't you?

MRS: I thought I did. Noah, what is a flood?

NOAH: That's what happens when it rains a lot.

MRS: Rains? Noah, you're talking Greek. What is rain?

NOAH: It's water that pours out of the sky. It's going to rain, and the rain will flood the earth. Only those in the ark will be saved. God is sick of this wicked, filthy world, and He's going to wash it clean.

MRS: Well, I can't blame Him for that. But, Noah, are you sure you heard Him right?

NOAH: Positive.

MRS: Noah, honey, sit down over here. I knew you had been taking your responsibility too much to heart. You can't save the whole world, you know. You've just got to get away and rest. Like I said, why don't we take a cruise?

NOAH: And like I told you, Mrs., we *are* going to take a cruise . . . in the ark I am going to build.

MRS: Noah, why don't you lie down for a while? Come. I'll give you a glass of warm milk.

EXIT BOTH.

SONG: "Noah Found Grace in the Eyes of the Lord" (chorus)

ENTER MR. AND MRS. NOAH. Noah carries a blueprint.

MRS: Okay, Noah. I believe you. It is going to rain and everyone not in your ark is going to drown. Knowing what kind of a carpenter you are, I just hope those in the ark don't drown too. Let me see the plans.

NOAH: *(unrolls blueprint)* Here it is. Exactly like the Lord told me. The architect did a good job, didn't he? Fifty cubits wide and thirty cubits high.

MRS: We ought to be able to get quite a few people in it.

NOAH: Ahhhh . . . ahhhhh . . . ahhhhh, honey, there's one thing I've neglected to tell you.

MRS: Yes?

NOAH: Well, you see, the Lord said . . . ahhhhh, the Lord told me . . .

MRS: Come on. Let's hear it.

NOAH: Well, we've got to take some animals in this ark, too.

MRS: Of course, we'll take Bossy and Fluffy and Tag. We'll need the chickens, too—if you can find time to build a pen for them. We can't have them running all over the place.

NOAH: We have to take some of every kind.

MRS: Every kind?

NOAH: Every kind!

MRS: Pigs?

NOAH: Pigs!

MRS: Lions?

NOAH: Lions!

MRS: S-s-s-snakes?

NOAH: Snakes!

MRS: Noah, this is ridiculous. The lions will eat the pigs, not that I'd mind that too much, but the snakes will bite the kids. And what if a skunk gets in your ark?

NOAH: That's to be expected, my dear. That's to be expected!

MRS: This gets sillier all the time. I doubt if anyone besides our family will even want in this floating zoo.

NOAH: Maybe not, but I have to do what God said.

MRS: *(looks at plans)* Here's the front door, but, Noah, where's the back one?

NOAH: There isn't one.

MRS: Only one door?

NOAH: Only one door!

MRS: What's this up there at the top?

NOAH: That's the window.

MRS: Oh, a skylight. How cute. They're very popular right now. We must be going to use solar energy. Where are the other windows?

NOAH: There aren't any.

MRS: No more windows? Now, Noah, I know you are super energy conscious, but only one window? What about ventilation? Surely God thought about the smell! Besides I'll get cabin fever if I can't see out. I've got to know what's going on around me.

NOAH: You might be happier not knowing. This is God's plan. We must build it according to His blueprint.

MRS: Well, you might at least point out to Him that He forgot the windows. How do you plan to pay for this ark?

NOAH: Well, I'll do most of the work so we won't have to pay anything for labor.

MRS: What about the materials?

NOAH: I guess I'll have to get a loan.

MRS: Ha! Who in the world would loan you money for a project like this?

NOAH: I don't know. Since you're so smart, how do you propose we pay for it?

MRS: I've been thinking I could help.

NOAH: You haven't any money.

MRS: But I can make delicious peanut brittle.

NOAH: What's that got to do with building an ark?

MRS: Do I have to spell it for you? M-O-N-E-Y.

NOAH: Oh, money! Oh, yeah! Now I see.

MRS: I also know how to make all kinds of pretty gadgets and doodads.

NOAH: Now see here, Mrs., you're not going to clutter up my ark with a craft sale.

MRS: M-O-N-E-Y, M-O-N-E-Y. Get it?

NOAH: I get it.

MRS: Now haven't you something to do? I have a lot to do.

NOAH: I could go see the planning commission about a building permit.

EXIT NOAH

MRS: Say, Noah, don't forget to ask God about the windows. *(to self)* I might enjoy this building project more than I thought. Now what should I do first?

EXIT MRS. NOAH

SONG: "Noah Found Grace in the Eyes of the Lord" (verse three)

ENTER NOAH, carrying hammer, and MRS. NOAH, carrying a clip-board and pencil.

NOAH: Well, there she is, honey. Took a little longer than I expected. But it's finished. Isn't she beautiful?

MRS: Know what I see when I look at that ark, Noah?

NOAH: Souls . . . lots of souls saved from the wrath of God.

MRS: That's what you see. I see 396,486 bags of peanut brittle, eighty-eight afghans, 419—

NOAH: Honey, I'm ashamed of you. You're so carnal.

MRS: Come on. Let's load up. I'll check off the animals as they board. But I'm warning you, Noah, those skunks had better stay on their side of the boat and behave themselves . . . or they'll be extinct!

NOAH: Okay. I'll take care of the skunks. Here comes our children. Let them get on board first.

EXIT MR. AND MRS. NOAH

SONG: "Noah Found Grace in the Eyes of the Lord" (last verse and chorus)

ENTER MR. AND MRS. NOAH

NOAH: Well, Mrs., do you think it was worth it?

MRS: Yes, Noah. It was. We didn't save everybody, but we did save our family. And by saving our family, we saved the world.

NOAH: I'm proud of you, honey.

MRS: Why? For all the money the ladies auxiliary raised?

NOAH: Because you didn't wipe out the skunk population.

MRS: There's one thing that bothers me a little bit, Noah.

NOAH: And what's that?

MRS: Well, I really hate to say it because it sounds so carnal, but . . .

NOAH: But what?

MRS: Well, it's this . . . in years to come when some historian writes up this event, I doubt if he will even mention the ladies auxiliary.

SONG: "Noah Found Grace in the Eyes of the Lord" (chorus)

EXIT MR. AND MRS. NOAH

SKIT

Mrs. Skinflint's Surgery

CAST: Lady Doctor, Nurse, Patient

PROPS: sewing kit, knitting needles, scissors, miscellaneous sewing items, carving knife, masking tape, magnifying glass, doctor's mask and coat, nurse's coat and cap, chair, large red bandanna

ENTER DOCTOR and NURSE, dragging a very reluctant PATIENT.

PATIENT: Let me go! I tell you there's nothing wrong with me!

NURSE: Oh, but there is. Isn't there, doctor?

DOCTOR: Absolutely. Absolutely. Now just settle down. We aren't going to hurt you.

PATIENT: But I'm not sick! I'm not sick!

DOCTOR: But you are sick. Anyone who won't give to Mothers Memorial has to be sick.

NURSE: That's right. You're a very sick woman.

PATIENT: I'm in perfect health.

NURSE: But you're not. You're sick, I tell you.

DOCTOR: And we intend to find the cause of your selfishness, Mrs. Skinflint.

Arguing continues as DOCTOR and NURSE wrestle PATIENT into a chair and hold her there.

DOCTOR: Hand me the tape, nurse.

NURSE digs in the sewing kit and brings out a roll of masking tape. They tape PATIENT's mouth shut. She struggles and mumbles.

DOCTOR: Hand me the needle, nurse. We've got to settle her down.

NURSE pulls out a knitting needle and hands it to the DOCTOR. She stands with her back to the audience and pretends to give the patient a shot. PATIENT immediately goes to sleep, sagging in the chair and snoring loudly.

NURSE: Finally!

DOCTOR: Yes, Mrs. Skinflint is one difficult case. This is an emergency. We need to do exploratory surgery immediately.

NURSE: *(squeals)* Oh, I'm so excited. This is my first case since I got out of nursing school.

DOCTOR: What a coincidence. It's my first case, too.

NURSE: What kind of surgery are you going to do, doctor.

DOCTOR: Why brain surgery, of course. That's got to be the problem area. Hand me the scalpel, nurse.

NURSE hands the DOCTOR a carving knife. Again she stands in front of the patient, back to the audience, and pretends to cut.

NURSE: *(squeals and covers her eyes)* Oooohhh, I think I'm going to faint. I can't stand the sight of blood.

DOCTOR: Don't be silly. You can't get blood out of a turnip.

NURSE gives a big sigh of relief and uncovers her eyes. They move behind the patient and pretend to probe inside her head.

DOCTOR: Now where is that brain? It's got to be here somewhere. Hand me a magnifying glass.

NURSE hands one to the DOCTOR, who peers at patient's head.

NURSE: She may not have one . . . anyone who won't give to Mothers Memorial can't have much brain.

DOCTOR: Ahhhhh, here it is. My, my, it's the smallest one I've ever seen. Of course, it's the only one I've ever seen.

NURSE: Let me see *(takes magnifying glass and peers into head).*

DOCTOR: Now we must be very, very careful, nurse. You do realize that the brain is an exceptionally delicate organ.

NURSE: Of course, I know that. *(points inside patient's head)* What's that strange little thing?

DOCTOR: *(looks closely)* Oh, that's the sob knob. It's an intricate part of the brain. It controls the tears ducts and grieving apparatus. When anything touches this area, it causes extreme grief.

NURSE: Really? This right here? *(pokes her finger into the patient's head)*

PATIENT sobs and chokes uncontrollably.

NURSE: Don't cry, Mrs. Skinflint. The doctor didn't mean to hurt you.

DOCTOR: The doctor? You're the one who touched the sob knob. Quick! Get the tape off her mouth before she chokes!

NURSE removes tape from patient's mouth. PATIENT continues to sob and cry. DOCTOR and NURSE try to console her.

DOCTOR: Turn it off, nurse. Turn it off!

NURSE: What?

DOCTOR: The sob knob!

NURSE: *(probes patient's head)* I can't find it . . . ahhhhh, there it is.

NURSE hands patient a large red bandanna. PATIENT blows her nose and promptly goes back to sleep.

NURSE: Whew! That was scary.

DOCTOR: Please, be careful! Remember we are dealing with a delicate organ.

Surgery continues for several seconds.

DOCTOR: *(points inside head)* That, nurse, is the laufatatus instigatus. It is the center that controls laughter. To touch it would send the patient into spasms of—

NURSE: You mean this thing right here. *(reaches over and pokes patient's head)*

PATIENT goes into spasms of laughter, almost falling out of her chair. DOCTOR and NURSE bring out various tools trying to stop her. Every time they touch her head, she laughs harder. Then they start laughing. When they are laughing so hard they stop touching the patient's head, the patient goes back to sleep.

NURSE: Wow! That was wild!

DOCTOR: We still haven't found the problem. Please, nurse, be very, very, very careful.

NURSE: *(points inside head)* What's that?

DOCTOR: That's the motor control center. Say—that could be the answer. If we could get her hands loosened up, she would work and give to Mothers Memorial.

They probe around on PATIENT'S head, causing her to do crazy things, like stick out her tongue, jerk her head, raise her eyebrows. NURSE encourages DOCTOR to keep trying until she finds the right spot. Suddenly the patient's hands start flying everywhere. They get so wild the nurse and doctor have to move out of the way.

NURSE: *(sadly)* Still no money.

PATIENT settles down. DOCTOR and NURSE move back to patient's side.

DOCTOR: Be careful, nurse. This motor control center is extremely touchy. This part controls the leg—

PATIENT jumps up and starts out.

DOCTOR: Mrs. Skinflint, come back! Come back! We haven't found the problem.

PATIENT stops at a safe distance and looks warily back.

NURSE: Doctor, I know where the problem is. It's not her brain. Everything in her brain is working. It's her heart. Her arteries are clogged. If something could touch her heart, she would work and give. She needs open heart surgery.

PATIENT: Oh, no! You're not going to do that to me!

PATIENT runs from the room with DOCTOR and NURSE in hot pursuit.

SPEAKER

Ask someone who has been the beneficiary of Mothers Memorial to be the guest speaker. Or if this is not possible, ask someone who has been a promoter and supporter of Mothers Memorial.

6

Music Notes

Speaking to yourselves in psalms and hymns and spiritual songs, singing and making melody in your heart to the Lord (Ephesians 5:19).

DECORATIONS: Use musical instruments, old sheet music and song books, music stands, and music boxes. Make music notes of black or gold paper and mount on the wall.

FAVORS: Tear pages from an old song book and decoupage on parchment paper, wallpaper samples or scraps of wood. Trim with bits of ribbon and dried flowers.

Copy a music score and use as clip art to decorate the programs.

SONGS: "In My Heart There Rings a Melody," "Let's Sing a Song about Jesus"

PUZZLE

Take Note

(Copy this music puzzle onto your programs. Let guests work on it while waiting for the banquet to begin.)

What musical term do these illustrations represent? Write your answers in the boxes.

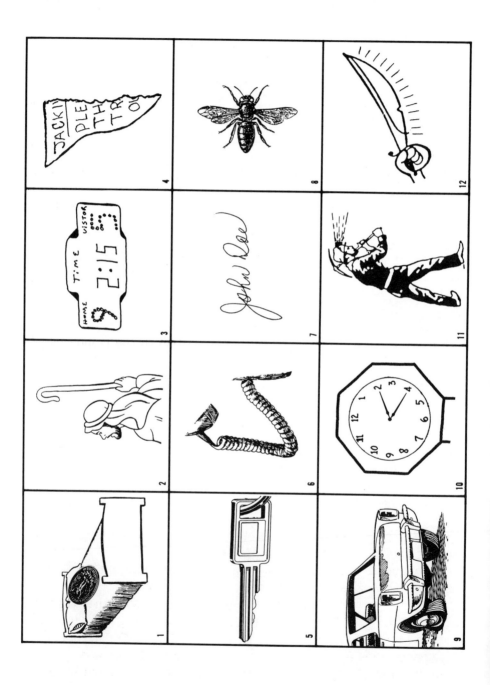

[ANSWERS: 1. a quarter rest 2. staff 3. score 4. a quarter (or half) note 5. key 6. (A) chord 7. signature 8. B 9. (A) flat 10. 2/4 timing 11. (A) minor 12. sharp]

RIDDLES

Each riddle should be answered with the name of a musical instrument.

1. What musical instrument makes a good pet? (trumpPET)
2. What instrument is part of the body? (ear/DRUM and/or ORGAN)
3. What was Alexander Graham Bell's favorite instrument? (saxaPHONE or xyloPHONE)
4. What instrument is associated with math? (PIano)
5. What instrument is a dog's favorite? (tromBONE)
6. What is the stickiest instrument of all? (guiTAR)
7. What instrument is used for bathing? (TUBa)
8. What instrument do cows prefer? (CORNet)
9. What musical instrument did the hobo carry? (BAGpipes)
10. What musical instrument did the driver of the Honda play? (ACCORDion)

GAME

An Ear for Music
Name That Instrument/Song/Artist

Pretape different musical instruments, songs, or recording artists, picking up snatches of songs from tapes.

Give guests pencils and paper and challenge them to identify the instruments, songs, or artists as the tape is played.

Or if music boxes are used for decorations, before the banquet make a list of the boxes and the songs they play. Ask guests to wind them so each is ready to play. At a given signal, all boxes are opened. With pencil and paper in hand, guests roam around the room, identifying the songs. Or if it is not convenient for players to move around, the songs may be played one at a time.

Award the winner a music tape or a music box.

ACTIVITY

Let's Make Music

Announce that you are going to start a band. Players may use anything around them except musical instruments. Two pencils become rhythm sticks. A comb and tissue make a yazoo. A glass of water and spoon make a handbell.

Choose simple songs everyone knows and ask someone to be the director.

Award prizes for the most unusual instrument, the loudest, the sweetest sounding, etc.

MUSICAL MONOLOGUE

And There Was Music

(To be presented dramatically with a background of music.)
Imagine, if you can, a world without music.

"No music?" the teen's mother might exclaim, "Wonderful! Blessed quietness."

But wait. Remember. There is no music—no scale, no tones, no pitch, only a monotone. So a mother cannot exclaim, "Wonderful!" She can only say, "wonderful."

In a world without music everyone speaks in a monotone. *(Strike one note and hold until directions change.)* One voice cannot be identified from another. Emotions are hidden in a deadly, level monotone.

What would the world be like without music? Canary or crow, the sound would be the same. Baby or grandfather, the voice would not tell. Major or minor, there would be no difference.

Blessed quietness? No. Not quietness. Dull, deafening noise.

But, thanks be to our heavenly Father, when He designed this universe, He desired more than noise for His children. So God ran His fingers up and down the Milky Way *(a run on the keyboard)* and out swept melodious tones that rode the air waves into the hearts of people.

(Soft, uplifting music) God wanted His children to hear and feel the thrill of life. He wanted them to dance and sing and skip and laugh. He wanted them to play in harmony, to march in step, to work in agreement. So He created music.

Music comes from the heart. It speaks to the soul. And it can control the mind.

Music calls men to war. *("Battle Hymn of the Republic")* It pulls them from recliners, office desks, assembly lines, lake shores, and from the arms of their loved ones onto the battlefields. Music puts courage in their backbones, fight in their hands, and excitement in their feet. Music gives soldiers strength, keeps them marching—and believing—when body and spirit are drained. Music frightens the enemy—for a marching army is a victorious one. *(Sing chorus.)*

Music soothes aching bodies, broken hearts, and fretful babies. *("Jesus Loves Me")* Music takes the hand of the weary, tormented soul and leads her beside still waters. It gently touches the fevered brow and whispers, "Peace. Be still." Music drives away the dark, haunting fears of memory and replaces them with the light of love and hope.

To the listening heart music is heard in the whispering breeze, the rushing waterfall, the giggling baby.

Music . . . God's loving arms wrapped around His children. Music . . . God laughing with His family. Music . . . God's gift to His creation. *("How Great Thou Art")*

7

Reflections

*But we all, with open face beholding as in a glass
the glory of the Lord, are changed into the same image
from glory to glory* (II Corinthians 3:18).

DECORATIONS: Use mirrors everywhere. Mirror tiles are a wise investment, as they can be used in many ways and places.

FAVORS: Give copies of *Reflections* magazine rolled and tied with ribbon. (Copies of past issues are available at a reduced price. Send your request to Ladies Auxiliary, United Pentecostal Church International, 8855 Dunn Road, Hazelwood, MO 63042 or call 1-314-837-7300.)
For door prizes and awards give gift subscriptions to *Reflections.*

ACTIVITIES

Mirror Images

I. Sign In

As guests enter, give each a slip of paper and pencil. Ask them to write their name or social security number in "mirror image" *(backwards).* Provide a hand mirror so they can check their writing. It must be written so that it appears correct in the mirror. *(Have extra slips of paper available. Some will have to try several times before getting it right.)*
Place papers in basket for a drawing later.

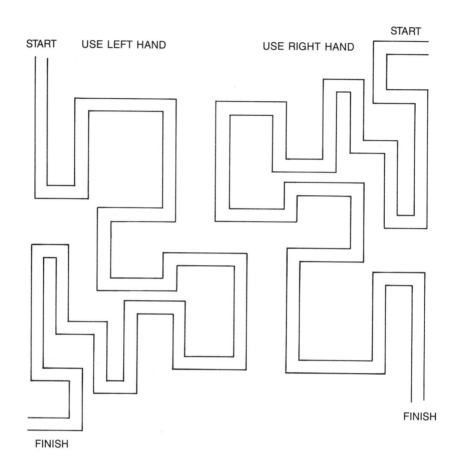

II. The A-mazing Mirror

Make a copy of this maze for each person attending. Each timekeeper will need a pencil, paper, and a stopwatch. On a table place a trifold mirror with the maze in front of it and a fine tipped marker beside it.

After guests have signed in, instruct them to go to this area. Set up one table for each twenty to twenty-five guests.

Place someone at each table to give instructions and keep time.

Instructions: As quickly as you can, looking in the mirror only, draw a line following the maze from start to finish, staying within the lines.

Do not touch or cross the "guidelines."

Do not look at the paper.

Follow the image in the mirror.

Each player's time is recorded.

68

Award the player completing the maze in the shortest time a prize. In case of a tie, have a drawing.

III. Simon Looks in the Mirror

To limber everyone up physically and socially, play a reverse game of "Simon Says." Instruct players to do as you, except they are to portray the mirror image. This will cause a lot of hilarity as players try to reverse their thinking and actions.

PUZZLE

Image Makers

(Place this icebreaker on the program. Ask guests to be working on it before the program begins and during the dinner.)
Find someone who has each feature and ask them to autograph your paper. The same person can only autograph your program twice.

1. Two people with eyes the same color.
   _____ and _____
2. Two people who are within two inches of the same height.
   _____ and _____
3. Two people with hair fixed in the same style.
   _____ and _____
4. Two people with the same kind of teeth.
   _____ and _____
5. Two people who are within three years of the same age.
   _____ and _____
6. Someone with the same Spirit as Christ.
   _____
7. Someone with the hands of Christ.
   _____
8. Someone with the mind of Christ.
   _____
9. Someone who speaks the words of Christ.
   _____
10. Someone with the heart of Christ.
   _____

SKIT

In Whose Image?

CAST: Mother, wearing old-fashioned clothes, Narrator

PROPS: rocking chair, newborn-size doll wrapped in blanket, copies of parts and instructions for speakers, name tags

INSTRUCTIONS: This skit can be produced with very little preparation and no practice.

Large name tags are worn around the neck to identify members of the Martin and Parson families. Make five name tags for even numbers: *Proud to be a PARSON,* and five for odd numbers: *MARTINS are best.*

The Narrator and Mother are the only ones on the platform. A copy of the script is on the podium for the Narrator. The speakers remain at their tables.

As guests enter, choose ten ladies to be the speakers. Give each one a name tag and a copy of her part along with these instructions.

Instructions for Speakers:

Put on your name tag immediately to create curiosity about the skit. Odd-numbered speakers are members of the Martin clan. Even-numbered speakers belong to the Parson family.

Watch the Narrator.

When she holds up finger(s) designating your number, stand and dramatically say (or read) your part, loud enough for all to easily hear. Then quickly sit down.

Speaker one starts calmly and slowly. Each speaker picks up in intensity and speed, until speakers nine and ten jump up like popcorn and shout their parts.

When the Narrator holds up a clinched fist, stand and shout out a paraphrased version of your first part. For example: "I tell you she's a Martin (or Parson), through and through." "She looks exactly like Aunt Sadie!" etc.

ENTER MOTHER, *carrying doll in blanket, sits in rocking chair. Starts rocking and singing, "Jesus Loves Me."*

NARRATOR: Ahhhhh, yes, a new baby, pure, innocent, adorable. A mother's joy, a father's pride, a family's conversation piece . . . *(holds up fingers, designating speakers).*

FIRST SPEAKER: *(stands)* Maggie's new little one looks just like the Martins. Why, when I looked at that baby, I saw Aunt Sadie, plain as day. *(sits)*

SECOND SPEAKER: *(stands)* Have you seen the new baby, little Mary Margaret? She has my Grandfather Parson's eyes, crystal blue. *(sits)*

THIRD SPEAKER: *(stands)* I knew the minute I saw Maggie's baby that she was a Martin. Got her dad's nose, sure as the world. *(sits)*

FOURTH SPEAKER: *(stands)* Oh, isn't Maggie's baby precious? She's a blue-eyed, blonde-headed angel, just like all Parson babies. *(sits)*

FIFTH SPEAKER: *(stands)* Little Mary Margaret's a Martin through and through. Even got Martin fingers. *(sits)*

SIXTH SPEAKER: *(stands)* Well, she has the Parson's toes. *(sits)*

SEVENTH SPEAKER: *(stands)* She's her father's spitting image . . . a true Martin. *(sits)*

EIGHTH SPEAKER: *(stands)* Mary Margaret looks exactly like her mother Maggie did when she was born . . . a Parson, if ever I saw one. *(sits)*

NINTH SPEAKER: *(stands)* I say she looks like Uncle Elmer . . . not a tooth in her head! *(sits)*

TENTH SPEAKER: *(stands)* Well, she's got the Parsons' gums! *(sits)*

NINTH SPEAKER: Who'd want the Parsons' gums? *(sits)*

NARRATOR holds up clinched fist. SPEAKERS jump to their feet and start shouting at one another.

NARRATOR: Enough! Enough! Ladies, please be seated.

SPEAKERS stop shouting and sit down.

NARRATOR: So at birth the compliments abound. Everyone thinks the baby looks like "someone"—in *their* family.

EXIT MOTHER with baby.

NARRATOR: As the child grows, the image becomes more distinct—at least, in the eyes of the beholder.

SPEAKERS stand to speak, then sit down.

FIRST SPEAKER: I've never known a child to be potty-trained so fast—well, not since Aunt Sadie was a baby.

SECOND SPEAKER: She gets her sweet disposition from the Parsons.

THIRD SPEAKER: Little Mary Margaret certainly is intelligent, just like the Martins.

FOURTH SPEAKER: Well, I wouldn't say that. Remember, it was a Parson who was valedictorian at Central High in '37.

NARRATOR: Then comes adolescence and we notice a not-too-subtle change in opinions.

FIFTH SPEAKER: I've never seen a more stubborn kid in my life. She must get that from the Parson side.

SIXTH SPEAKER: Dumbest kid I ever saw. Not a brain in her head. Just like her Grandpa Martin.

SEVENTH SPEAKER: Clumsiest girl I ever saw. Wonder if she needs glasses. Most of the Parsons are nearsighted.

EIGHTH SPEAKER: Is she ever going to learn to act like a lady? She reminds me of her Grandmother Martin, as brassy as they come.

NINTH SPEAKER: Still reminds me of Uncle Elmer—never hears a word you say!

TENTH SPEAKER: Mary Margaret's more Martin than I ever dreamed! It's a pity, too. *(sighs heavily; says slowly and distinctly)* She was such a sweet baby.

EXIT NARRATOR

SPEECH OUTLINE

Christ's Reflection

Christ shall be magnified in my body, whether it be by life, or by death (Philippians 1:20).

The only Christ many people will see is what they see in "Christians" like yourself. What kind of an image are you portraying to the world?

Develop an illustrated talk to enlarge upon this theme, using several mirrors.

1. a cracked one (a distorted image)
2. a dirty one (a blurred image)
3. a tarnished one (a tainted image)
4. a clean, clear, magnifying one

By our actions we either magnify or belittle Christ in the eyes of the world.

Let the world see Jesus in you.

8

The Land of Make Believe

Except ye be converted, and become as little children, ye shall not enter into the kingdom of heaven (Matthew 18:3).

DECORATIONS: Create a toyland in your banquet hall. Gather stuffed animals, dolls, doll houses, storybooks, etc. If space is limited, use only one kind, such as dolls or antique toys. Scatter confetti on the tables to create a fairyland effect.

Place a brightly colored sign on the door: "Welcome to Make Believe Land. Drop your troubles at the door."

FAVORS: Give each guest a party toy.

PUZZLE

Thinker-Toys

(Copy this mind boggler on the program for a prebanquet filler.) Each definition describes a toy. How many can you identify?

1. a part of the ear _____
2. to send a package by rail _____
3. to endure _____
4. a blast; a good time _____
5. a type of dirt _____
6. to perplex _____
7. to record charges on police blotter _____
8. easily moved _____
9. part of a goat's head _____

10. to expand or swell out   _____
11. to teach   _____
12. to exchange; barter   _____
13. to act silly   _____
14. to stop passage   _____
15. to ransack or plunder   _____

[ANSWERS: 1. drum 2. ship 3. bear 4. ball 5. clay 6. puzzle 7. book 8. mobile 9. horn 10. balloon 11. train 12. truck 13. clown 14. block 15. rifle]

GAME

Fairy Tales

Before the banquet, go to the library and scan fairy tales and Mother Goose books for names of characters. Write each one on a slip of paper. Place in a basket.

Give each player a pencil and an 8 by 11 1/2 inch sheet of paper that has been folded and divided into sixteen squares. On each table place a bowl of jelly beans.

Before or during the meal, the player writes the names of sixteen characters from fairy tales or Mother Goose rhymes on her paper, one name per square.

To play, the leader tosses the names in the basket and draws them out one at a time. As a name is called, the players look for that name on their paper. If it is there, they place a jelly bean on it. The first player to cover every name on her paper wins.

ACTIVITY

Just Imagine

Imagination is a gift from God that children know how to use better than adults.

Allow a few minutes for mothers to share funny things their children have said or done while using their imaginations.

SKIT

Annie Body

CAST: Narrator, Annie Body, Stepmother Fear, Stepsister Inferiority, Stepsister Ignorance, Fairy Godmother

PROPS: name tags, rod, tinsel for Fairy Godmother's hair

ENTER FAIRY GODMOTHER, ANNIE, FEAR, INFERIORITY, and IGNORANCE (in that order). They stand in a line with their backs to the audience. As each one's name is called, she turns and curtsies to the audience.

NARRATOR: Once upon a time, not too long ago and not too far away, there lived a young lass named Annie Body. Annie lived with her wicked stepmother, Fear, and her stepsisters, Inferiority and Ignorance.

Poor Annie! Fear, Inferiority, and Ignorance constantly harassed and abused her.

ANNIE listens in horror to the abuses hurled upon her and shrinks away from the others.

FEAR: You? You go to the King's banquet? Why, you can't go! You know you're afraid to stick your head out of your shell!

INFERIORITY: How can you ever think about going to the King's wedding supper? You know you're not worthy. Why, you're a nobody.

IGNORANCE: You wouldn't know how to act. You'd fall flat on your face.

FEAR: Yeah! What if someone spoke to you? Oh, horrors! You know you couldn't possibly carry on a conversation with anyone intelligent.

INFERIORITY: Everyone else will be dressed in lovely clothes. You don't have a decent thing to wear.

IGNORANCE: You're so stupid you wouldn't know which fork to use and you're sure to spill iced tea all over the person sitting beside you.

ANNIE: Stop! Stop! I know I can't go to the King's wedding supper. *(sobs)* I know I'm not pretty enough or smart enough or charming enough. But that doesn't stop me from wanting to go. Oh, go away, all of you! Get out and leave me alone!

FEAR, INFERIORITY, IGNORANCE move to one corner, laughing and chanting, "You can't go. You're too dumb. You can't go. You're too dumb." They stand watching.

NARRATOR: Poor Annie Body. How she wanted to go to the King's wedding supper. The invitation had said everyone was invited. But she was soooo afraid and felt soooo inferior and soooo ignorant. She began to play her favorite game, "If Only."

ANNIE: *(sighs)* If only I had expensive clothes like Natalie, I would be pretty. *(sighs)* If only I had a personality like Cheryl, I would be popular. *(sighs)* If only I was rich like Julie, I would be happy. *(sighs)* Oooohhhhh, if only . . .

NARRATOR: Enter Fairy Godmother.

FAIRY GODMOTHER, holding a rod, turns and curtsies to the audience.

ANNIE: *(jumps up in fright and cowers)* Oooohhh! Who are you?

GODMOTHER: Do not be afraid, my child. I am your fairy godmother.

ANNIE: *(squeals and claps her hands)* My fairy godmother? Oh, wonderful! You have come to wave your magic wand over my head and give me expensive clothes like Natalie's and a personality like Cheryl's and money like Julie's! Then I will be pretty and popular and charming and I can go to the King's wedding supper.

GODMOTHER: You can be pretty and popular and charming and go to the King's wedding supper.

ANNIE: Oh, hurry! Hurry! Wave your magic wand and say the magic word.

GODMOTHER: Discipline!

ANNIE: What? What did you say?

GODMOTHER: I said, "Discipline." The magic word is "discipline."

ANNIE: *(looks at self)* But it didn't change me. I know what's wrong. You didn't wave your magic wand. Wave your wand, Fairy Godmother. Try again.

GODMOTHER: I can't change you, Annie. Only you and God can do that. Here I will give you this. *(hands rod to Annie)* It is not a magic wand. It is the rod of "discipline."

FEAR: Don't give that to her.

ANNIE: Just looks like an old stick to me.

GODMOTHER: Discipline is not pretty, but it is a very important part of our lives, Annie. To be pretty, charming, and popular, you must use this rod daily. You must discipline yourself to think of others, to be polite and caring . . . then you will be charming and popular. You must discipline yourself to eat a balanced diet, exercise properly, and take care of your appearance—then you will be healthy and sparkling. You must discipline yourself to pray and study God's Word. When you have a right relationship with your Creator, you will be happy.

FEAR: Don't tell her that!

ANNIE: But I want you to do it for me.

GODMOTHER: I can't. You must do it for yourself.

ANNIE: Ooooh, but I'm afraid I can't do that.

FEAR, IGNORANCE, INFERIORITY: *(chant)* You can't do it. You're too dumb. You can't do it. You're too dumb.

GODMOTHER: Stop it! Annie, you must drive Fear, Inferiority and Ignorance out of your life! You must stop saying, "I am afraid. I can't do it!"

FEAR, IGNORANCE, INFERIORITY: But she can't. She can't.

GODMOTHER: Instead, Annie, you must say, "I can do all things through Christ who strengthens me."

FEAR, IGNORANCE, INFERIORITY: No! Don't say it! You'll kill us! Don't say it!

GODMOTHER: Say it, Annie. "I can do all things through Christ who strengthens me."

ANNIE: "I can do . . ."

FEAR, IGNORANCE, INFERIORITY: No! You can't.

ANNIE: "I can do all things . . ."

FEAR, IGNORANCE, INFERIORITY: *(weaker)* No. No. You can't do that to us.

ANNIE: "I can do all things through Christ who strengthens me."

FEAR, IGNORANCE, INFERIORITY: *(stumbling from the room, yelling grow weaker and weaker)* Stop! Don't say that! You can't. You're too dumb. You can't . . .

EXIT FEAR, IGNORANCE, and INFERIORITY.

ANNIE: *(holds rod above head)* "I can do all things through Christ who strengthens me." I can discipline myself. I can be happy. I can be charming. I can go to the King's wedding supper.

EXIT ANNIE and GODMOTHER.

SPEECH OUTLINE

Our Wonder-full World

I. Seeing through a Child's Eyes
   A. Everything is wonder-full.
   B. Everyone is perfect.

II. Responding as a Child
   A. Trusting and forgiving
   B. Worshiping with delight

III. Becoming like a Child
   A. Depending on our Father
   B. Enjoying our world

SONG: "Lord, We Depend on You"

9

The Quilting Bee

That their hearts might be comforted, being knit together in love (Colossians 2:2).

DECORATIONS

The Quilt Booth

Turn the banquet hall into a giant quilt booth. Encourage ladies to enter their quilts in your fair by offering nice prizes. Set a deadline for several days before the banquet for entries. This will allow time for arranging the display and judging.

Ask two or three people in your community unrelated to your group to serve as the judges. Consider asking a seamstress, the owner of a craft store, and a professional lady. In appreciation for their services, give the judges free tickets to your banquet (an excellent way to introduce them to your church).

Prizes could be awarded for the following quilts: (1) oldest, (2) best stitched, (3) most unusual, and (4) prettiest. Allow time during the banquet for presentation of the awards.

FAVORS: Hot glue a silk flower and bow to the top of spool of thread. Give one to each guest.

QUIZ

A Quilting Quiz

(Copy this quiz on programs.)
What quilting terms or materials contain the following words?

0. Placed on a door for safety   b̲ [l] [o] [c] [k]
1. A nickname for Patrick   [ ] [ ] [ ] _ _ _ _
2. A kind of tree, also remains in a fireplace   _ [ ] [ ] [ ]
3. A nocturnal flying mammal   [ ] [ ] [ ] _ _ _ _
4. A dish   _ _ _ [ ] [ ] [ ] [ ] [ ]
5. A brand of detergent   [ ] [ ] [ ] _ _ _
6. What you do to books   _ _ [ ] [ ] [ ] [ ]
7. A male sheep   _ [ ] [ ] [ ] _
8. A type of metal   [ ] [ ] [ ] [ ]
9. A billboard   _ _ [ ] [ ] [ ] [ ]
10. A lawn   [ ] [ ] [ ] [ ]

[ANSWERS: 1. PATtern 2. sASH 3. BATting 4. temPLATE 5. FABric 6. thREAD 7. fRAMe 8. IRON 9. deSIGN 10. YARD]

GAMES

Piece Work

Make a copy of the fan block given here for a pattern. Cut on solid lines into eight pieces.

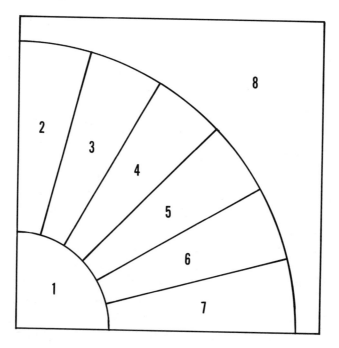

Using color-coordinated wrapping paper or cloth, cut each fan piece (2-7) from a different design. Pieces 1 and 8 are solid color. (Each block is the same.) You need one block per eight ladies, plus one for display. Assemble one block by gluing or tacking it to a cardboard base. Place the other pieces in a basket and toss.

As ladies enter, let each choose one piece.

When it is time to play, display the finished pattern. Ladies are to find the other seven pieces required to make one block. The ones who piece together the first complete block are the winning team. Give each a package of needles.

MONOLOGUE

My Memory's Fine

PROPS: two telephones, cane, Bible, comfortable chair, two small tables

INSTRUCTIONS: Set-up requires small table with a Bible on it beside a chair. Across the stage is another table with the telephone on it.

A toy telephone that has a realistic ring is needed for the sound effect. Someone stands to one side or behind the scene and rings it at the appropriate time.

ENTER MOLLIE, hobbling on cane. Sits down, drops cane, and picks up Bible. Her glasses are perched on the end of her nose. A copy of script is hidden in the Bible.

MOLLIE: Time for Bible reading. Let's see where am I? *(leafs through the pages)* Ahhhhh, yes, here I am—Psalm 88. "O LORD God of my salvation, I have cried day and night before thee."

I shore have. Why I've seen enough trouble in my day to make old Job think he'd been on vacation. *(yawns)*

Now, let's see where was I? *(leafs through the pages again)* Oh, yeah, here I am—Psalm 88. "O LORD God of my salvation, I have cried day and night before thee."

Might as well cry all night. Can't sleep with Hilda snorin'. I shore do miss Bert. He never snored like that. It was bad enough spending my first childhood with Hilda, now I've got to spend my second one with her. Guess we should be thankful we've got each other. Lots of widders ain't got nobody, not even bossy sisters.

Now, let's see where was I? *(leafs through the pages again)* Oh, yeah, here I am—Psalm 88. "O LORD God of my salvation, I have cried . . ."

Seems to me like I've read that before. Must have read it yesterday. Think I'll drop on down here and read. . . . *(yawns widely)*

"Shall thy wonders be known in the dark? and thy righteousness in the land of forgetfulness?"

The land of forgetfulness . . . know lots of folks who live there! Hilda, fer one. She can't remember her first husband's name half the time. Calls him Albert. Everybody knows that was her third husband.

Now me, there ain't nothin' wrong with my memory. My memory's fine. Why, I can remember them good ole days like they was yesterday. *(yawns)*

I remember the time Bert and me and Hilda and Albert or was it George, anyway . . . I remember . . . the time . . . we all took the kids and . . . *(mumbles, dozes, almost drops Bible, snorts, straightens).*

Now, let's see, where was I . . . *(peers at Bible)*. Oh, yeah, in the land of forgetfulness. I mean, Hilda was there. Why I remember the time we . . . *(falls asleep and begins snoring loudly).*

SOUND: TELEPHONE, continues to ring until Mollie answers it.

(Snorts and wakes) That telephone! Ever' time I get to havin' my devotional time, it rings. *(staggers to her feet, taking her Bible with her and pushes her glasses up on her head)*

I'm a-comin'. I'm a-comin'. *(looks around for cane)* Now where's that cane? Ahhhhh . . . here it is.

(Leans on cane and starts across the room) Now where was I a-goin'. Oh, yeah, to get a drink of water. Shore am thirsty.

Why, the phone's a-ringin'. Might as well answer it since I'm up. Now where is that phone? *(yells)* Helen? Henryetta? Hettie? Now what is her name? Oh, yeah, Hilda! Hilda! Where'd you put the phone? She must have her hearin' aid turned off again.

Ahhhh, here's the phone. *(picks up receiver)*

Hello . . . hello. What? Is this 225-0680? Just a minute and I'll see. *(lays down receiver)* Now where's my glasses? How'm I'm gonna see what number this is if I cain't find my glasses? *(starts looking for them, shakes head, and glasses fall down on her nose)*

Ahhhh, there they are. *(picks up receiver)* Now what number were you callin'? 225-0680? *(holds receiver away from ear and peers at it)* Yes, ma'am, this is 225-0680.

Is Mollie Brown home? Just a minute I'll check. *(holds phone away from mouth and yells)* Mollie? Mollie Brown? Is there anyone here named Moll . . . Mollie? Oh, that's me. Of course, I'm home. *(to self)* Merciful day, what will that woman think of me?

(Puts receiver back to ear and disguises voice) Hello. Mollie Brown speaking. . . . What's that you say? You're offering a course on eight simple steps to improving your memory? Oh, that reminds me, I was goin' to get a drink. Excuse me, please. *(lays down receiver and start to leave)* Now where's my cane? That thing sure is a nuisance. Ahhhh, here it is. *(picks up cane)*

Well, looky there, the phone's off the hook. Hilda must'a been talkin' to someone. *(picks up receiver)* Hello? Yes, this is Mollie Brown. Lady, did you call me or did I call you? . . . You called me? Well, then what do you want?

You want to sell me a course in improving your memory? Lady, I don't need that. There ain't nothin' wrong with my memory. Why I remember when Richard Roosevelt was president. I dare say you can't remember that! . . . I thought not. . . . What'd you say? . . . Who's the president now? . . . It's ahhhh . . . it's ahhhh. . . . Listen, lady, if you don't know that you'd better take that course yourself.

What'd you say? . . . Just forget it? Why, lady, I'd be glad to. *(hangs up phone)*

Now, let's see where was I? Oh, yeah, I was readin' 'bout them poor folks in the land of forgetfulness.

(Mutters as she starts for door) Imagine her thinkin' I needed to take a class in child psychology. There's ain't nothin' wrong with my memory . . . if I could just remember where I put it!

EXITS

PANTOMIME

The Senior Saints' Quilting Bee

In this skit not one word is spoken, although players move their mouths as if talking. The implication is that each one is so deaf that she cannot hear a word that is said. Players signal this from time to time throughout the skit by placing a hand behind their ear and wrinkling their forehead, mouthing, "Speak up! I can't hear a word you're saying!"

Props *(with the exception of chairs)* are imaginary. Costumes and actions say it all. Use ladies who are uninhibited and dramatic.

Four young ladies dressed as old ladies gather at the home of one for a quilting bee.

They greet one another, then set up the frame and tack the quilt to it. This requires tugging and pulling, tacking and retacking. *(Probably they will have to be prompted by an older lady who knows how to do this.)*

As they are tottery, deaf and half-blind, the actions could be hilarious.

Finally, the quilt is in place. They put chairs in a square on each side of the "frame" and begin quilting. Remember, only the chairs are real. Passing the thread around, they thread their needles *(not an easy task for an old lady)* and begin sewing. One is not sewing straight and this upsets the others. Occasionally, a quilter sticks her finger with a needle. Encourage the cast to be creative and dramatic.

The scene ends when one looks at her watch and is shocked by the time. Three rush from the room, leaving the lady of the house with a mess to clean up.

SPEECH IDEA

Pieced Together

Use bits of fabric, needle, thread and a pattern to show how a beautiful life can be pieced together from scraps by the Master Designer.

Ask two ladies whose scattered lives have been made into something beautiful by Jesus Christ to give their testimonies.

Or use the same objects to illustrate how God takes individuals from different backgrounds and knits us together with the thread of love into a beautiful church.

SONG: "Something Beautiful"

10

Wash Day

Wash me, and I shall be whiter than snow (Psalm 51:7).

DECORATIONS: What else but old-fashioned rub boards? These may be purchased in several sizes at craft stores. Decorate with silk flowers and bows to coordinate with the color scheme. Use for centerpieces and door prizes.

FAVORS: Soap, of course. Homemade lye soap is best. Wrap in nylon netting, tie with ribbon, and add a silk flower.

If lye soap is not available, use decorator soaps in small baskets.

PUZZLE

(This thought provoker may be printed on the program for prebanquet time filler.)

How many of the thirty-six name-brand cleansing agents mentioned in this story can you find?

A Soap Opera

It was on the East Coast where Joy met her faultless love.

"Come, my dove," he said boldly. "Let us go surfing while the tide is right."

She smiled as he caressed her hand. "I get the dreft." She loved to be soft-soaped. As they bounced into the vivid blue waters, she shouted, "Be my life buoy."

"Yes, I will," he answered with zest, "if you will be my bride."

The wedding was fantastic.

Dawn found them standing in the sunlight at the foot of Niagara Falls as the waters cascaded over them. "It's like spray-n-wash," she whispered as she snuggled in his downy arms.

"This is the best yet," he sighed.

Home at last. She tackled the laundry cheerfully. "It's a cinch. In a wisk I'll have these clothes spic-n-span."

But as the first load came out of the washer, she ran for the phone to direct dial her mother. "Oh, Mom," she wailed.

"What's wrong, honey?" Mother asked. "Is the honeymoon era over?"

"It's fabulous . . . all I ever dreamed," the young bride cried. "But you didn't teach me how to do the laundry. My love now has six pairs of pink underwear!"

[ANSWERS: Joy, Coast, Faultless, Dove, Bold, Surf, Tide, Caress, Dreft, Softsoap, Bounce, Vivid, Shout, Lifebuoy, Yes, Zest, Fantastic, Dawn, Sunlight, Niagara, Cascade, Spray-n-Wash, Snuggle, Downy, Best Yet, Tackle, Cheer, Cinch, Wisk, Spic-n-Span, Direct, Dial, Era, Fab, All, Pink]

QUIZ

Bath Time

1. What lady in the Bible bathed in the Nile River?
2. Whose feet were bathed in tears?
3. Who was made clean by dipping in a muddy river?
4. Who said that in the good times he washed his feet in butter?
5. Who tried to cleanse his conscience by washing his hands?
6. Who didn't want his feet washed?
7. Whose backs were washed by a Philippian?
8. Who volunteered to be "a servant to wash the feet of the servants of my lord"?
9. Who was called in from the battlefield and told, "Go down to thy house, and wash thy feet"?
10. Who criticized the disciples because they did not wash their hands before they ate?

[ANSWERS: 1. Pharaoh's daughter 2. Jesus' 3. Naaman 4. Job 5. Pilate 6. Peter 7. Paul and Silas 8. Abigail 9. Uriah 10. the Pharisees]

GAME

Wash It

Give each player a pencil and paper. Allow three minutes for them to list as many items as they can that have to be washed. Answers may range from face to car to soul.

When time is called, ask for a volunteer to read her list. Players mark off of their lists any item named. Ask another player to read the items remaining on her list. Players mark these articles off their lists. Continue until no duplicate items are left. The winner is the one with the most items remaining on her list.

For a prize give a box of detergent or a decorated towel set.

SKIT

Hanging Out the Wash
(Mothers Memorial Promotional Skit)

CAST: Wilda, the washerwoman, Narrator

PROPS: basket, clothesline, clothespins, clothespin bag, coveralls, insulated underwear, dress, socks, corset/girdle, sweat shirt, slip, tie, shorts

INSTRUCTIONS: This skit is for a ladies-only audience.

All items are in the basket Wilda carries, except the clothespins and clothespin bag, which the Narrator has hidden in the podium.

ENTER WILDA, from back, breaking into the program. She is dressed in work clothes and an apron, wearing glasses, and carrying the basket of clothes.

WILDA: *(ad-libs, grumbling and complaining about wash day until she nears the front)* What in the world is going on here?

NARRATOR: That's what I'd like to know. What's going on? You are interrupting our program. Who are you and what are you doing here?

WILDA: You answer my question, then I'll answer yours.

NARRATOR: We're having a ladies banquet.

WILDA: Banquet? Humph! Just a bunch of women sittin' and gabbin' when there's work to be done. Let me get through here.

NARRATOR: Now answer my question. Who are you and what are you doing here?

WILDA: I'm Wilda the Washerwoman. And what am I doing here? You ought to be able to tell by lookin'. I'm hang—*(drops basket)* Oops! Well, can't you give me a hand? Wet clothes is heavy. Careful there! Don't get 'em dirty. Bet half you women sittin' here wastin' time have got dirty linen at home.

COMES TO FRONT, looks all around, then peers at women over edge of glasses.

WILDA: Now where's that clothesline? I declare half the women in this world ain't even got a clothesline anymore . . . got them new-fangled clothes dryers that toss and tear and wrinkle. . . . Downright dangerous things they are. Now where's that clothesline?

NARRATOR: We don't have a clothesline here.

WILDA: Just what I thought! So I came prepared. *(dips in basket and pulls out clothesline; picks two women out of the audience)* You and you—come up here. You get to be the clothesline poles.

WOMEN hold clothesline across front.

WILDA: Now let's get down to business. *(pulls coveralls from basket, starts to hang them on the line)* Oh, no! Ain't that stupid?

NARRATOR: What's stupid?

WILDA: I ain't got no clothespins. *(to audience)* Any of you society gals got clothespins in your purses? Just what I thought. They all got them wicked clothes dryers.

NARRATOR: Well, guess what, Wilda. *(holds up bag of clothespins)*

WILDA: *(scratches head)* There's something funny going on around here. How'd you know I would need clothespins?

NARRATOR: That's not too hard to figure out, if you think about it.

WILDA: Ain't got time fer thinkin'. Got to get these clothes hung out.

NARRATOR: Whose dirty laundry are you about to air?

WILDA: Dirty laundry? This ain't no dirty laundry. It's my Mothers Memorial wash.

NARRATOR: Mothers Memorial wash?

WILDA: Yep! *(hangs coveralls on line)* Mothers Memorial COVERS ALL needs. We send money to foreign missions, home missions, Harvestime, Tupelo Children's Mansion, the Boy's Ranch. Why you just name it . . . Mothers Memorial COVERS ALL.

NARRATOR: So I see. What else is in your basket?

WILDA: *(pulls out insulated underwear)*

NARRATOR: Insulated underwear? What in the world does that have to do with Mothers Memorial?

WILDA: We're getting this Mothers Memorial drive WARMED UP, ain't we?

NARRATOR: Well, if those won't warm it up, nothing will. Tell us more.

WILDA: *(pulls out dress)*

NARRATOR: A dress! Let me guess. We're going to DRESS up our program. Now what?

WILDA: *(pulls out sweat shirt)* Raising money ain't easy. Gotta SWEAT, ladies. Cain't do it sittin' here sippin' tea and actin' like high society. Gotta get with it! *(pulls out socks)*

NARRATOR: Socks?

WILDA: Well, certainly! Socks get dirty, too. *(puts one sock on fist, waves it in the air)* Come on, ladies, let's SOCK it to the devil this year . . . and raise more money than we've ever raised. If everyone gave more than ever, guess what? Our offering would be bigger than ever. Ain't that sharp thinkin'? *(hangs up socks)*

NARRATOR: Well, I don't know. There are so many special drives—Sheaves for Christ, Christmas for Christ, Save Our Children. . . . Is Mothers Memorial really a worthy cause?

WILDA: *(shakes finger at Narrator)* Now, now you just look here. *(pulls out and holds up corset)*

NARRATOR: A corset?

WILDA: COURSE IT'S a worthy cause!

NARRATOR: "Course it's a worthy cause?" Hummmm . . . prove it!

WILDA: For *($ amount)* you can support one of them there foreign Bible school students a whole term. A whole term, I tell you. Try sendin' your kid to school all year for *($ amount)*. And you get this neat little certificate with this guy's, or gal's, picture on it. Why, you won't find a bargain like that at Dillard's or even Wal-Mart.

NARRATOR: I guess not. Many of those Bible school students baptize hundreds of people in Jesus' name.

WILDA: Yep, and if you've sponsored 'em, who knows? You might get an extry diamond in your crown. Now where else can you get a diamond fer *($ amount)*? But what am I doin' standin' here a-gabbin'? I've got a laundry to hang out. *(pulls out slip)*

NARRATOR: Now what?

WILDA: Don't let the deadline SLIP up on you, ladies. Remember it's *(date)*. I'm almost finished. *(hangs up tie)*

NARRATOR: A tie? Did you wash your husband's tie?

WILDA: Naw! But how else can I TIE this crazy skit together? *(to ladies holding clothesline)* Raise it up! Higher! Higher! On tiptoe, ladies. Let's raise our Mothers Memorial goal higher and higher. Up and over! Over and out! *(starts to exit, looks in basket, comes running back)* Almost missed one thing. *(hangs shorts on line)* Guess what?

NARRATOR: I don't have to guess. I know.

TOGETHER: Don't come up SHORT!

EXITS

SPECIAL SPEAKERS

Instead of calling in a special speaker, ask ladies in your group who have experienced a miraculous cleansing of spirit to give their testimonies. Perhaps someone has received a baptism of forgiveness and now loves someone who inflicted great hurt on her. Another lady has been delivered from alcoholism or drug addiction. And don't overlook the ladies who have been cleansed from fear or pride or depression. This has the potential to be one of the best programs you have ever had.

These are they which came out of great tribulation, and have washed their robes, and made them white in the blood of the Lamb (Revelation 7:14).

Dramas

Synopses of Dramas

These dramas have been presented at the United Pentecostal Church Oklahoma District ladies retreats. The props are very simple. In most cases, provision is made for the cast members to carry hidden copies of the script because it is impractical to expect anyone to remember all the lines.

At the first rehearsal, the cast members become acquainted with their roles. A tape should be made of a reading of the script. This can be duplicated and each player given a copy. This memory aid is immensely helpful.

The second rehearsal emphasizes entrances, exits, voice inflections, positioning, etc.

The final rehearsal should be held at the retreat site a few hours before the services begins.

The scenes are designed to be presented throughout the retreat. Scene I introduces the theme during the opening ceremonies. The last scene is the wrap-up.

Stretching the drama out in this manner provides highlights throughout the retreat. Also, when the drama is split into three or four scenes, given a few hours apart, the cast can rehearse each scene shortly before it is presented. This clears the players' minds from the whole play and allows them to concentrate on each scene.

A Goodly Heritage

Do you long to see the glory of God in the sanctuary as it was in the "good ole days"? Have you ever prayed like Moses, "Lord, shew me thy glory"? If so, the message of this drama will speak to your heart.

Three visually impaired sisters, each declaring, "There's nothing wrong with my vision," gather memorabilia to take to the Church family reunion. In so doing, they take a trip into the past and meet some godly ancestors who give them new insights on the glory of God.

This drama would be excellent for an anniversary service, as well as a ladies retreat.

Approximate time: one hour, twenty minutes (four scenes)

A Role Play

Before we were born, God designed a role for us to play in life. Whether we fill our role or not is a decision we make. Only those who accept and fulfill their God-given role find true happiness and contentment.

This three-part drama moves the audience to laughter, and at unexpected moments, tears. It encourages women to yield to God's plan and cease struggling to be what they are not. It emphasizes the value of each role.

Approximate time: one hour

School Days

This hilarious allegory helps us see ourselves as others see us. In these days when our spirituality often is measured by how stressed out, heavy laden, and worried we are, we take a closer look at our burdens. Are we bearing the burden of the Lord or burdens we have manufactured to impress our classmates?

As Miss Comforter lightens the load of her weary, heavy-laden students, the viewers find their loads growing lighter as they laugh until they cry.

Approximate time: one hour, twenty minutes *(four scenes)*

The Race

Ever feel as if you are in a race with time? Perhaps that is because you are wasting time running from the past or worrying about the future.

In this three-act drama the Traveler makes peace with the Past and conquers Worry when she finds her lost friend, Joy, in the presence of the King.

Both cast and audience benefit from this play as they learn to slow down and enjoy the trip.

Approximate time: one hour

1

A GOODLY HERITAGE

Yea, I have a goodly heritage (Psalm 16:6)

CAST

The Church Sisters
    Bertha (Firstborn)
    Maybelle (Middle Child)
    Hillary (Youngest)
Ella Kilgore
Jewel Fauss
Jeannie Seymour

PROPS

Scene I:

microphone *(off stage for introduction)*
stacks of mail *(for each of three characters)*
    Bertha: bills, *Pentecostal Herald*, letter.
    Maybelle: junk mail, Harlequin novel, book mailer, letter.
    Hillary: miscellaneous, *Good Housekeeping*, magazine, letter,
    box of memorabilia, including photos of self and family.
three small tables
three chairs
three telephones
three photo albums
miscellaneous items for living areas *(magazines—relating to each
    one's taste; lamps, tablecloths, etc, include a pillow at
    Maybelle's house)*
telephone for sound

Scene II: same stage setup as for Scene I

medium box containing records, books and Bertha's photo album
larger box containing Hillary's records and photo album
handkerchief, crutches, overhead projector, projector screen,
   transparencies

Scene III: same stage setup and props as Scene II

Scene IV: no stage setup required

3 suitcases
microphone on side
handkerchief
Their Story: 20th Century Pentecostals

INSTRUCTIONS: All directions are given from the stage facing the audience.

Bertha is "far sighted." She holds everything at arm's length to see it. She is the boss of the family, very proud and conscientious. She glories in her "righteousness," and wants "holiness" to be preached in every service.

Maybelle has "cataracts." She is constantly squinting and shading her eyes to protect them from the light. She glories in her liberal-mindedness and wants "love" to be preached all the time. Every time she says "love" she rolls her eyes and sighs.

Hillary is "nearsighted." She holds everything close to her face. She's the scatterbrained family clown, very self-centered. She glories in self and wants to be in the spotlight all the time. She isn't interested in preaching, only "shouting."

Pentecostal pioneers mentioned in Scenes II, III and IV can be changed to include names of people familiar to your area. As the Church sisters look at photos, transparencies of them (made on a copy machine) are shown on an overhead screen, allowing the audience to view what the girls are looking at. Transparencies of Hillary's school photos may also be shown, if desired, or showing of transparencies may be completely omitted. Change the place and time of reunion to your retreat location and dates.

Responsive readings at the beginning of each scene are read by the audience to create a spiritual mindset correlating with the theme of the scene.

Characters should stand up and move around as much as possible to keep the scene moving.

Scene I

The Glory of the Past

STAGE SET-UP: Three living areas (table, chair, telephone, photo albums, magazines); one right (Bertha's house), one left (Hillary's house), and one center (Maybelle's). At Bertha's house everything is in perfect order. At Hillary's everything is a shambles. Maybelle's is livable.

RESPONSIVE READING

And [Moses] said, I beseech thee, shew me thy glory (Exodus 33:18).

Now when Solomon had made an end of praying, the fire came down from heaven, and consumed the burnt offering and the sacrifices; and the glory of the LORD filled the house. And the priests could not enter into the house of the LORD, because the glory of the LORD had filled the LORD'S house (II Chronicles 7:1-2).

So the spirit took me up, and brought me into the inner court; and, behold, the glory of the LORD filled the house (Ezekiel 43:5).

O God, thou art my God; early will I seek thee: my soul thirsteth for thee, my flesh longeth for thee in a dry and thirsty land, where no water is; to see thy power and thy glory, so as I have seen thee in the sanctuary (Psalm 63:1-2).

AUNT GRACE: *(off stage, mike on vibrato)*
Dear Ones:
I am writing to invite you to the Church family reunion. It will be *(Friday and Saturday, November sixth and seventh,)* at *(Fountain Head Lodge.)*
If you want a room in the lodge, you had better get your reservations in early. Our Church family is growing and it is getting harder and harder to find accommodations large enough for us.
Please bring any old photographs, records, letters, or memorabilia, you have that might be of value in compiling our family history.
Church folks are coming from near and far. You won't want to

miss this exciting family reunion.

Hoping to see you at *(Fountain Head)* soon.

Love,

Aunt Grace

ENTER BERTHA, from right, sorting through a large stack of mail, which is arranged in perfect order, according to size, singing, "When We All Get to Heaven." She holds each item at arm's length to read. She stumbles and almost falls several times over "imaginary" items, which she does not see.

BERTHA: *(begins talking when she reaches the mike)* Bills! Bills! Bills! At least, I guess they're bills. Why does everyone write in lower case, elite print?

Ahhhh, here's my favorite magazine. *(holds up the Pentecostal Herald)* I've been waiting all month for the *Pentecostal Herald*. How it feeds my soul!

Now, let's see . . . is there anything else besides bills? *(keeps trying to "stretch" arm so she can read)* Ahhhhh, this one feels a bit different. Why I believe it's a letter. *(Opens envelope, goes through all kinds of contortions, trying to read it. Finally, puts it on the floor, backs up 2-3 feet and nods.)* Well, now, that's better! *(fades out as she reads)*

"Dear Bertha: I am writing to invite you to the Church family reunion. . . ." *(sits down—later as Hillary talks, she kneels beside her chair)*

ENTER MAYBELLE, from back center (she has been sitting in audience up to this point). She is singing loudly, "Fill My Way Every Day with Love." Carries an armload of mail, staggers, gropes, and shades her eyes as she makes her way to the stage. Drops several pieces that she has trouble finding as she stoops to pick them up. Continues singing until she reaches the stage.

MAYBELLE: *(places mail on her table, pretends to turn lamp down)* This light is blinding me. There's not a silver lining behind every cloud for me, there's a rainbow around every light. These disgusting cataracts! But I WILL NOT HAVE SURGERY. I WILL NOT.

(Begins to sort through mail) I declare, the mailman must be the biggest junkie in town. . . . All the junk mail he carries, it's a wonder he's not got a ruptured vertebra.

(Picks up large mailing envelope) Ahha! My Harlequin romance of the month! Wonderful! I can't wait to read it. I just *love love* stories. *(sighs blissfully)*

(Picks up letter) What is this? It can't be! But it is! It's a letter! Imagine, someone writing a letter! Whoever would do a strange thing like that? *(Opens envelope. Twists and turns letter, trying to read it.)* Sure is fuzzy. Must have written it with a blurry pen. . . . Oh, it's typed. Well, the typewriter had a blurry ribbon. My cataracts can't be getting worse.

(Fades out as she reads haltingly) "Dear Maybelle: I am writing to invite you to the Church family reunion. It will be *(Friday and Saturday, November sixth and . . .)*"

ENTER HILLARY, from left. Has large pair of glasses pushed up on her head. Carries a helter skelter stack of mail, which she has trouble holding on to.

HILLARY: *(shouts, calling attention to herself)* Praise the Lord! Oh, what a beautiful morning. I just feel like shouting!

(Spins and skips; trips and stubs toe, shouts) OOOOHHHH! My toe! Ohohohoh! My poor toe! *(hobbles to stage, moaning and groaning)*

And it was such a beautiful day! Well, I've just got to praise the Lord anyway. I am determined no matter what trouble comes *my* way, *I'm* going to praise the Lord. I'm sure not going to be like Sister Wilma. She's been crying all month because her husband died.

Oooohhh! Praise the Lord for my aching toe.

(Gropes around) Now where is that table! I wish I could find my glasses. If those kids don't leave my glasses alone, I'm going to . . . *(trips on table or chair and stubs toe again)* OHOHOHHHHHH! MY TOE! MY TOE! *(weakly)* ohpraisethelord. MY TOE! *(slumps down into chair, moans subsiding)*. OHOhoh . . .

(Weakly) Well, what's in the mail? Probably nothing but junk advertisements and bills. *(holds Good Housekeeping magazine under nose)* Here's my *Good Housekeeping* magazine. Might as well cancel that subscription. I thought it would help me be a better housekeeper. Hasn't helped one bit. Course, I never remember to read it. *(throws magazine on floor)*

What's this? A letter? *(handles gingerly)* It's a real-live letter? *(Rips open. Holds close to nose. Reads.)*

Dear Hillary:

I am writing to invite you to the Church family reunion. It will be *(Friday and Saturday, November sixth and seventh,)* at *(Fountain Head Lodge.)*

If you want a room in the lodge, you had better get your reservations in early. Our Church family is growing and it is getting harder and harder to find accommodations large enough for us.

Please bring any old photographs, records, letters, or memorabilia you have that might be of value in compiling our family history.

Church folks are coming from near and far. You won't want to miss this exciting family reunion.

Hoping to see each one of you at *(Fountain Head)* soon.

Love,

Aunt Grace

(Tosses letter into the air, lets fall to the floor) Whoopeee! Wonderful! Two heavenly days away from Jake and the kids . . . and this house! *(gropes around)* I've got to call the girls. I know they'll want to go. Now where is that telephone? That's what I hate about these newfangled portable phones. They're never in the same place twice . . . And neither are my glasses. . . . Oh, here's the phone. Now what's Bertha's number? I think it's 2-2-5-4-3-0-3. *(picks up phone, holds it close to her face and dials)*

SOUND: *BUSY SIGNAL*

HILLARY: Busy. She's probably talking to Maybelle—about me! Big sisters straightening out little sister! I just know they're upset because I was late for church last night. I'll just call Maybelle and tell her to mind her own business. *(dials)* 2-2-5-0-6-8-0.

SOUND: *TELEPHONE RINGING*

MAYBELLE: *(picks up phone)* Hello?

HILLARY: Maybelle, is that you?

MAYBELLE: Who else would it be?

HILLARY: I mean, are you home?

MAYBELLE: No. I've gone shopping.

HILLARY: I want to know what you and Bertha were saying about me.

MAYBELLE: Which time?

HILLARY: Just now, on the telephone.

MAYBELLE: I haven't been talking to Bertha on the telephone.

HILLARY: Well, you certainly have. Bertha's line was bus . . . *(covers mouth with hand)* Oooooohhhh, what's my number?

MAYBELLE: Honestly, Hillary. Don't you even know your own number?

HILLARY: Why should I? I never call myself. Is my number 2-2-5-4-3-0-3?

MAYBELLE: It is. Why?

HILLARY: I just called myself, and the line was busy. I wonder who I was talking to?

MAYBELLE: Oh, Hillary! Why did you call me?

HILLARY: I called to find out what you and Bertha were saying about me. But you weren't talking about me. If you weren't talking about me, who were you talking about?

MAYBELLE: We weren't talking! Now if you'll excuse me, I've got to look through my pictures and see what I want to take to the reunion.

HILLARY: Oh, that's why I called. I just got the most exciting news. We're having a family reunion at *(Fountain Head Lodge.)*

MAYBELLE: I know, Hillary. I got a letter from Aunt Grace, too.

HILLARY: Dear old Aunt Grace. What would the Church family do without Grace? Are you going to the reunion, Maybelle?

MAYBELLE: Didn't you just hear me say I have to decide what photos I'm taking?

HILLARY: If you're going through your photos, I think I'll bring mine and come over. Call Bertha and see if she wants to come over, too. But don't you talk about me! *(hangs up phone, grabs photo album)* Now where are my glasses? *(tears things apart looking for them—turns her back to audience and stands still)*

MAYBELLE: *(mimics Hillary)* "I'm coming over. Call Bertha." That's just like Hillary. It's never "May I come over?" or "Why don't you come over?" No doubt, her house is in shambles. *(dials phone)*

SOUND: *TELEPHONE RINGING*

BERTHA: *(jumps up from knees, looks at watch, answers phone)* Hello?

MAYBELLE: Bertha, did you get a letter from Aunt Grace?

BERTHA: Yes. But, Maybelle, you are interrupting my prayer time. Don't you know I always talk to our Father in the mornings?

MAYBELLE: Oh, I'm sorry, Bertha. I forgot. But since you are on the phone, you might as well talk to your sister. Are you going to the family reunion?

BERTHA: Oh, no, definitely not!

MAYBELLE: Why not?

BERTHA: Because I've gained five pounds in the last year. I could *never* let everyone see me like this, especially not Aunt Grace!

MAYBELLE: But, Bertha, Aunt Grace wants you to come. She doesn't expect you to be perfect. She just wants you to come.

BERTHA: No, no, I can't do it! I'd be humiliated the whole time. It makes me so mad to think I allowed myself to get this sloppy! Besides why did Aunt Grace have it at *(Fountain Head)?* Some of us don't have that kind of money.

MAYBELLE: But you just bought a new car.

BERTHA: That's why I don't have that kind of money. And besides I'm terribly busy.

MAYBELLE: Very well. Stay home. Hillary just called and—

BERTHA: Why was she late for church last night?

MAYBELLE: I don't know. She didn't say. Back to the reunion—Hillary and I are going. We're going to look through our photographs and family mementos to see what we need to take for the history book. We thought you might want to come over and help us, but if you're not going to the reunion—

BERTHA: Who said I wasn't going? I'm sure I can dig up the money somewhere. And if I fast three days and diet the rest of the time, I should get rid of this flab by the *(sixth)*.

MAYBELLE: Then are you coming over?

BERTHA: *(looks at watch, holding it at arm's length)* Well, I really don't have time . . . but I suppose I'd better come. I have three minutes and sixteen seconds left in my prayer hour. After that, I'll be over. *(hangs up phone and stands up)* I wouldn't go, but there's no telling what those two will decide to take to the reunion if I'm not there to help them. Let's see . . . three minutes and sixteen seconds . . . That's about enough time to pray for the lost. I've already prayed about the important things. *(kneels beside chair)*

HILLARY noisily gathers up her photo album and pulls her chair over to Maybelle's. As she does so, she stubs her toe again and makes a great commotion about it, all the while expressing her determination to "praise the Lord" in spite of such great adversity. Maybelle tries to comfort her. Finally gets her settled in her chair. Hillary continues moaning and crying.

ENTER BERTHA, carrying photo album and bringing her chair.

BERTHA: Child, what in the world is the matter with you?

HILLARY: Oh, Bertha, I stubbed my toe! Three times this morning I've stubbed my toe!

BERTHA: If you'd wear your glasses, you could see where you're going.

HILLARY: I would if I could find them. *(straightens up, leans toward Bertha and points at her)* You're a fine one to talk about wearing glasses.

BERTHA: But I don't need glasses.

HILLARY: Ha!

BERTHA: Besides glasses make me look old.

HILLARY: You mean, older!

MAYBELLE: Girls, don't fuss.

BERTHA: *(to Maybelle)* And when are you going to have surgery?

MAYBELLE: I'm not! There's nothing wrong with my vision that I can't live with. It's a little cloudy, but I always did like cloudy days.

HILLARY: *(starts to stand up, falls back in chair, moaning)* Oh, my toe. Pray for me, Bertha.

BERTHA: I will . . . tomorrow morning when I have my quiet time.

HILLARY: Tomorrow morning?! I need prayer now.

BERTHA: Have you talked to our Father this morning?

HILLARY: Not yet. I planned to as soon as I got the kids off to school. Then I got this letter from Aunt Grace and—

BERTHA: Don't expect me to do your praying for you, young lady. It's time you grew up and took responsibility for your own actions. You stubbed your toe. You pray for it!

MAYBELLE: Girls! Don't you *love* each other? That's the problem with this family today. There's not enough *love* in the Church. I remember how it was back when I was a child. Everybody loved everybody!

BERTHA: I doubt that. But I'm sorry, Hillary. I forget that you're a grown woman.

HILLARY: That's okay, Bertha. I'm pretty touchy sometimes.

MAYBELLE: That's better. Perhaps that wonderful sermon Brother Pastor preached last night on *love* is bearing fruit.

BERTHA: That reminds me. Why were you late last night, Hillary?

HILLARY: It's none of your bus—

MAYBELLE: Girls! *Love* one another. Oh, how we need more preaching on *love*.

BERTHA: I think we need more preaching on holiness. The last good holiness sermon I heard was five months and three weeks ago. I remember when I was a little girl, Grandmother Church dressed HOLY!

MAYBELLE: Oh, Bertha, don't be so old-fashioned. In this enlightened generation, we know it's what's on the inside that's important.

HILLARY: I say we've already heard enough preaching to save the world; we need to shout and rejoice! I remember hearing the old-timers tell about dancing around the wood stove until midnight. I don't know why we don't see things like that in our services today.

MAYBELLE: Could be because we don't have wood stoves.

HILLARY: Very, very funny.

MAYBELLE: There was a lot of shouting last night after Linda Luke received the Holy Ghost. If you hadn't left early, you could have shouted to your heart's content. I didn't get home until 11:30.

BERTHA: I know one thing—this Church family isn't what it used to be! And I'm not talking about shouting around wood stoves. I don't know what is going to happen to the next generation when *we're* gone!

MAYBELLE: Seems like I remember hearing Grandmother Church say the same thing about us.

BERTHA: I don't know why she would worry about *us*. There's nothing wrong with *us*. It's the next generation that has me worried. I shudder to think what is going to happen when *they're* in control.

HILLARY: You're just a worry wart, Bertha. Relax. As long as there is peace and prosperity in my day, that's all I'm concerned about. Let the next generation do their own worrying. That's my motto . . . and the government's too.

BERTHA: *(looks at watch, jumps up)* Dear me! Look at the time! I've got to run. We'll have to look at these albums later.

MAYBELLE: Let's meet at your house after dinner, Bertha.

BERTHA: My house? Oh, no. I just ran the sweeper and every time someone takes a step on the carpet, it leaves a footprint.

MAYBELLE: *(sighs heavily, stands up)* All right. Let's meet at your house, Hillary.

HILLARY: *(jumps up)* Oh, we can't do that! My house is—

ALL: IN SHAMBLES!

MAYBELLE: I might have known. Okay, we'll meet here at my house right after dinner.

BERTHA and HILLARY, pick up their albums and EXIT. MAYBELLE lingers behind long enough to find her Harlequin romance, which she tucks under her arm. She sighs contentedly and EXITS, singing "Fill My Way Every Day with Love."

Scene II

The Glory of Suffering

STAGE SETUP: Same as in Scene I

RESPONSIVE READING

Then he said unto them, O fools, and slow of heart to believe all that the prophets have spoken: ought not Christ to have suffered these things, and to enter into his glory? (Luke 24:25-26).

And if children, then heirs; heirs of God, and joint-heirs with Christ; if so be that we suffer with him, that we may be also glorified together. For I reckon that the sufferings of this present time are not worthy to be compared with the glory which shall be revealed in us (Romans 8:17-18).

But rejoice, inasmuch as ye are partakers of Christ's sufferings;

that, when his glory shall be revealed, ye may be glad also with exceeding joy (I Peter 4:13).

For our light affliction, which is but for a moment, worketh for us a far more exceeding and eternal weight of glory (II Corinthians 4:17).

ENTER MAYBELLE, from back, holding a Harlequin paperback (containing script) in front of her nose, singing "Fill My Way Every Day with Love." Sways and staggers as she comes down the aisle, but is so engrossed in her book she doesn't notice. Takes a seat at the table in her house. Reads a few seconds, then starts to sniff and cry. Takes out handkerchief and blows nose.

ENTER BERTHA, from right, carrying a box filled with papers (with script in open photo album on top). Stops to peer at her watch. Shakes head, sighs and frowns as she heads for Maybelle's house (center stage) in a very businesslike manner.

BERTHA: I really don't have time for this nonsense. Oh, the sacrifices I make for this family . . . my energies, my time, my money . . . *(enters Maybelle's area, places box on table)* Hello, Maybelle. Helloooo, May-belllle?

MAYBELLE: *(without looking up, sniffs)* Hi.

BERTHA: Is Hillary here? Why in the world are you crying, Maybelle?

MAYBELLE: *(chokes)* Oh, it is just so sad. There is so much heartache and suffering in this world!

BERTHA: You're right about that—drug addiction, abortion, AIDS, divorce . . .

MAYBELLE: *(wails)* Divorce—Stacy is threatening to divorce Delbert just because she found—

BERTHA: Stacy? Delbert? Who are they?

MAYBELLE: *(looks ashamed)* Well, they . . . they . . . they're this couple in this book . . .

BERTHA: Maybelle! Come back to the real world. Isn't there enough suffering in real life? It's a wonder you're not blind . . . sitting here reading in the dark!

MAYBELLE: You worry about your eyes, and I'll worry about mine!

BERTHA: There's nothing wrong with *my* eyes, but you know your cataracts are getting worse. When are you going to have surgery?

MAYBELLE: I told you . . . I'm not. I can live with things being a little fuzzy and cloudy. And a rainbow around lights never hurt anyone. *(shudders)* I'm not about to let them start cutting on my eyes! Pain just kills me. You know I never did like to suffer.

BERTHA: Who does? But it's just a simple little procedure with a laser—a beam of light.

MAYBELLE: *(shudders more violently, cries)* I know all about it. It has to hurt. I can't stand a tiny bit of dust in my eye, much less a powerful beam of light. Besides I can't stand the light. I'm much more comfortable in semidarkness. So don't start nagging me about corrective surgery. While we're on the subject, when are you going to get glasses?

BERTHA: I don't need glasses. THERE'S NOTHING WRONG WITH MY VISION. I've had 20/20 vision all my life.

MAYBELLE: You mean the first forty-five years of your life. You're either going to have to get glasses or add an extention to your arm.

BERTHA: If we're going to look through this stuff, we need to get started. I'm a busy woman. Where's Hillary?

MAYBELLE: *(shrugs)* You know Hillary. She'll probably get here about the time you're ready to leave.

BERTHA: *(picks up photo album and holds it at arm's length)* Do you know who this is, Maybelle? It looks kinda like one of Grandmother Church's nephews and his wife.

MAYBELLE: *(squints)* Looks pretty hazy to me. They didn't have very good cameras back then, did they?

ENTER HILLARY, on crutches, one foot wrapped in a stuffed white sock. She is trying to carry a large box filled with family "memorabilia" (script in album on top). Finally, she has to put the box down and push it with her foot. She forgets and pushes it with her "sore" foot. Carries on like she is dying. Girls run to her side. (NOTE: Girls need to memorize lines from this point until they open their album.)

BERTHA: What happened, Hillary? Did you break your foot? Oh, you poor dear!

HILLARY: OhpraisetheLord! Help me get to a chair. Why do I have to do all the suffering?

MAYBELLE: Did you have an accident, Hillary? Why didn't you call us?

BERTHA: If you'd wear your glasses, you wouldn't have so many accidents.

HILLARY: I told you, I can't find my glasses.

GIRLS ad-lib as they get Hillary seated comfortably with her foot propped up on a pillow. Hillary moans about how much she is suffering.

BERTHA: Now tell us what happened.

HILLARY: I broke my toe . . . I think.

BERTHA: You think? Did you have it X-rayed?

HILLARY: No . . .

MAYBELLE: Have you been to the doctor?

HILLARY: No . . .

BERTHA & MAYBELLE: How do you know it's broken?

HILLARY: I don't know . . . I told you, "I think it's broken." Remember, I stubbed it three times . . . four times today! *(sobs)* It's been a terrible day. *(shakily)* Praise the Lord.

MAYBELLE: Praise the Lord?

HILLARY: *(clinches teeth, strongly emphasizing "I")* I am determined, I've made up my mind, I'm going to praise the Lord . . . no matter how much suffering, how much pain, how much humiliation . . . I'm going to praise the Lord . . . even if I have to do it through clinched teeth. I'm going to praise the Lord.

MAYBELLE: I'm not sure our heavenly Father gets much glory out of that kind of praise.

HILLARY: Oh, yes, He does. It's when you praise Him through clinched teeth that He gets the most glory.

MAYBELLE: Seems to me like He would get more glory out of a heart full of *love* than clinched teeth.

BERTHA: The way we really give glory to God is by living a godly, holy life.

HILLARY: You give God glory your way, I'll give Him glory mine. But how can I dance and run and shout with a broken toe? *(sighs)* Oh, well, I'm sure God understands. What were you girls doing?

MAYBELLE: Looking at these old pictures. Do you recognize this couple?

HILLARY: *(holds photo under her nose)* I wish I could find my glasses. *(puts photo down and opens her photo album)* But it doesn't really matter. What we need for the family history book are up-to-date pictures. Here's a picture of me playing the piano at my first recital. And here's another of me when I was twelve and I played Mary in the Christmas drama. And here I am again giving the salutatory address at my graduation.

BERTHA: I thought you said we needed "up-to-date" pictures.

MAYBELLE: That's not what Aunt Grace wants, Hillary. She wants to trace the roots of the Church family.

BERTHA: You're not a root, Hillary. You're just a little limb, a pretty showy one, but nevertheless a little one.

HILLARY: You will have to admit that I was *very* popular in school.

MAYBELLE: *(peers at photo again)* These people look familiar. Bertha, you ought to remember. You're the oldest.

BERTHA: Just by two years, three months, and six days! *(places photo on floor and backs up)*

HILLARY: *(aside to Maybelle)* But *she* doesn't need glasses.

OVERHEAD: PLACE ON SCREEN PHOTO #1 (BROTHER AND SISTER DEAL).

BERTHA: They do look familiar. *(snaps fingers)* Why, that's Brother and Sister Deal. No wonder, I didn't recognize them. I was trying to remember our ancestors—you know, ancient history!

MAYBELLE: Brother and Sister Deal aren't that old, but they are an important part of the Church family history. *(sighs)* Brother Deal, bless his heart. He is just the sweetest guy, so kind to everyone.

HILLARY: And Sister Deal is extra special.

BERTHA: Yes. No one knows, not even their closest friends, all they have sacrificed and suffered for this Church family.

HILLARY: No one knows what they've suffered? Why don't they tell someone? If I suffer I want the whole world to know.

BERTHA & MAYBELLE: We know!

BERTHA: *(points out another photo)* Who is this young couple?

HILLARY: Let me see. *(holds under nose)* Hummm . . . they sure do look familiar!

PUT TRANSPARENCY #2 (BROTHER AND SISTER NELSON) ON OVERHEAD

MAYBELLE: *(squints)* Could that be . . . yes, I believe it's Brother and Sister C. A. Nelson.

HILLARY: My, but we have pretty ladies in the Church family. I'm sure I resemble Sister Nelson or Sister Deal. *(preens)* They look so . . . so . . .

MAYBELLE: Blurry!

HILLARY: Oh, Maybelle, that's your cataracts. Actually, they look clean and fresh and glowing.

BERTHA: It's the beauty of holiness. I pray we never lose it, but sometimes I wonder . . .

MAYBELLE: *(sarcastically)* Oh, don't get started on that, Bertha.

BERTHA: *(sighs)* The Nelsons sacrificed a lot to preach the gospel. But you'd never know it to hear Brother Nelson. He makes jokes about their hardships.

HILLARY: To hear him tell it, wearing cardboard in your shoes and praying for a three-cent stamp was fun.

BERTHA: I guess it's all in how you look at it. *(slowly and thoughtfully)* Yes, it's all in how you look at it.

MAYBELLE: I believe it's called "having a right perspective."

BERTHA: *(points out another photo)* Do you recognize this couple?

PUT PHOTO #3 (BROTHER AND SISTER LYONS) ON OVERHEAD.

MAYBELLE: *(peers over Bertha's shoulder)* Oh, I know who they are—Brother and Sister Lyons, Sister Bass' parents. Remind me some day when we have more time to tell you about them. It's a beautiful love story.

BERTHA: I declare Maybelle I think you're lovesick!

MAYBELLE: *(ignoring Hillary, points at another photo)* This is Brother and Sister C. P. Kilgore. Wonder what miraculous stories they could tell?

PUT PHOTO #4 (BROTHER AND SISTER C. P. KILGORE) ON OVERHEAD.

ENTER ELLA LEE KILGORE. GIRLS are shocked.

SIS. KILGORE: I could tell of many, many times when God miraculously healed us. I could relate numerous times when He wonderfully supplied our needs.

But instead, girls, I want to talk about a faith, a trust in God, that goes deeper than mountain-moving faith. It is faith that knows when God does not move the mountain, He will take our hand and help us climb it. It is that quiet, unwavering trust that says, "Not my will, but Thine be done"—a faith that is strengthened by suffering.

While we were in Friendship, Arkansas, my husband felt led to go to Paris, Texas, in search of a revival. He found one and came back for us. All clothing, cleaning, and cooking necessities, along with five children, my husband, and me were loaded into the Kilgore car.

When we arrived in Paris, we lived with one of the saints until we could find our own place. While we were there, the saint's children came down with the measles.

Brother Kilgore found us a house . . . it wasn't much, but it was ours. We were barely settled when . . . one by one . . . the children had the measles. In fact, they prayed to get sick because the "sick" ones got candy.

R. G., the oldest boy, about fourteen at this time, found a job and turned all his earnings over to his dad for the family.

There was very little food and I was nursing baby Paul. When he caught the measles, they settled in his bowels. Hour after hour I rocked my baby and prayed. Odetta, who was ten, did the washing and ironing. As little Paul grew weaker and weaker I rocked and prayed . . . rocked and prayed. Surely God would not let my baby die. Weren't we doing the work of the Lord? Weren't we in the will of God? Didn't we spend hours every day in prayer? Surely God would not . . .

But He did. Baby Paul died.

Blinded by tears, I washed and dressed my baby for the last time.

My husband begged a box from a store to build a little pine coffin. We lined it with a quilt I had made, and we buried our baby in the pasture.

After the simple funeral, we went back to our barren little home. I walked around the empty rocking chair, through a curtain hanging across a corner, into my prayer closet. And there I stayed until faith spoke. Yes, we were doing the work of God. Yes, we were in the will of the Lord. Yes, our heavenly Father still loved us, and His ways are right. The peace of God flooded my soul. I was ready for my next mountain—whether it moved or I had to climb it was not important. I was ready.

I suppose you think I sacrificed and suffered. Perhaps, I did, but it was strange . . . I never thought of it like that. The blessings of the Lord made us rich. We had God. We had one another. And we had truth. We were rich . . . we were blessed.

Let me tell you about one of my riches. I had very little formal education. Reading and understanding God's Word was difficult for me. But every time I picked up the Bible, an angel of the Lord stood at my side and read to me. Imagine an angel for a tutor! I was rich.

Our children grew up, married and moved away. Eventually, I became very sick—stomach cancer. The doctor gave me ninety days to live.

We moved our little travel trailer to Modesto, California, to be near Odetta and her husband, Horace. Every morning Horace came, coffee in hand, to visit with me. In spite of the intense pain in my body, I had peace in my soul and a smile on my lips.

Then the enemy came. "Your salvation is not real. You've wasted your life. Where's your God now?"

I did the only thing I knew to do. I prayed. For days I prayed. Then my wonderful Lord took me to a river, a sparkling river. On the other side the air seemed purer, the grass greener. Oh, how I wanted to cross.

The next day as I lay in my bed, my frail body wasted and racked with pain, my Father led me across that river. When Horace came, I told him, "I've made it! I've made it over the river! It is so beautiful!"

Horace went for Odetta. She gave me my bath, dressed me, and sat holding my hand.

Then Jesus came and stood at the foot of my bed. Oh, what glory filled the room! And what a conversation we had! All Odetta heard was my replies, "Oh, yes. Oh, yes. Oh, yes."

Then He gently took me by the hand and together we entered glory. The sufferings were not worthy to be compared to the glory that awaited me. My light affliction worked for me a far more exceeding and eternal weight of glory.

The same glory is waiting for you, if you, too, will "count it all joy."

EXIT ELLA LEE

SONG: "Whatever It Takes"

EXIT GIRLS

Scene III

To God Be the Glory

STAGE SETTING: Same as Scenes I and II.

PROPS: Same as Scenes I and II, Transparencies 5-7

INSTRUCTIONS: ENTER GIRLS quietly, take places at table during the responsive reading. Hillary on crutches.

RESPONSIVE READING

It is not good to eat much honey: so for men to search their own glory is not glory (Proverbs 25:27).

But God forbid that I should glory, save in the cross of our Lord Jesus Christ, by whom the world is crucified unto me, and I unto the world (Galatians 6:14).

That no flesh should glory in his presence (I Corinthians 1:29).

Give unto the LORD the glory due unto his name; worship the LORD in the beauty of holiness (Psalm 29:2).

For thine is the kingdom, and the power, and the glory, for ever. Amen (Matthew 6:13).

MAYBELLE: We're finding some strong roots in our family tree.

BERTHA: Yes, and we've barely started. *(picks up album)*

HILLARY: You know, girls, there's no telling who—or what—we would see *if* we could see. I wish I could find my glasses.

PUT PHOTO #5 (BROTHER A. D. URSHAN) ON OVERHEAD.

BERTHA: *(points at photo)* That's Brother A. D. Urshan, a great man of God.

MAYBELLE: I remember hearing about him. *(counts off on fingers)* He was the father of our general superintendent, Brother Nathaniel Urshan. He wrote many marvelous articles and books. He carried the truth of Jesus' Name baptism to Iran and Russia.

HILLARY: Wow! I wish God would use me to carry the gospel to some foreign country . . . like Hawaii.

MAYBELLE: Hawaii isn't a foreign country, Hillary.

HILLARY: Well then, Bermuda would do.

MAYBELLE: What a consecration!

BERTHA: I imagine Brother Urshan was so proud that poor common saints like us couldn't get within ten feet of him.

MAYBELLE: Bertha! What a terrible thing to say! He was a man of God full of *love* and compassion.

BERTHA: *(counts off on fingers)* If I had preached in foreign lands and wrote marvelous articles and had a prominent son, I'd be proud!

MAYBELLE & HILLARY: WE KNOW!

HILLARY: No doubt, we would have to make appointments to see you. Maybe that's why you've never *(counts off on fingers)* preached in foreign lands or written marvelous articles or had a prominent son. Great men are never proud men.

BERTHA: Wow! I'm impressed. I didn't know you had such depth, Hillary. "Great men are never proud men."

MAYBELLE: I've been told that when Brother Andrew Urshan worshiped, it was as if he was a subject standing before a throne. He came in great humility, aware of the awesome presence of the King.

PUT PHOTO #6 (BROTHER O. F. FAUSS) ON OVERHEAD.

BERTHA: Let's move on, girls. *(points at picture)* This is Brother O. F. Fauss.

MAYBELLE: I wish they had focused those cameras better.

BERTHA: I wish you'd have surgery for those cataracts.

MAYBELLE: When you get glasses, I'll have surgery.

HILLARY: Girls! Remember—

BERTHA & MAYBELLE: We know. *Love* one another.

MAYBELLE: Hey, that's *my* line!

BERTHA: Brother Fauss served as assistant general superintendent of the United Pentecostal Church for many years. He was—

ENTER JEWEL FAUSS

SISTER FAUSS: He was a wonderful husband, a loving father, and a true man of God.
     The first time I saw Oliver Fauss, I was peering through a knothole in the wall of my uncle's house. We girls were watching the young Pentecostal preachers go down the road to the big brush arbor where they were holding a revival. It was 1916 in DeQuincy, Louisiana. I told my cousins, "The one with one of his britches legs rolled up is mine."

MAYBELLE: *(squeals)* Ohhhhhh, another *love* story!

BERTHA: Hush, Maybelle! Listen.

SISTER FAUSS: And he *was* mine. About four months later we were married . . . Jewel Eleanor Smith became Jewel Eleanor Fauss. We put all our belongings in one suitcase. We preached anywhere we were asked and stayed anywhere we could.
     Once I had a terrible earache and needed hot water for my water bottle. The lady of the house where we were staying would not let Oliver build a fire in the cookstove. He had to build a fire in the back yard to warm the water.
     One time I needed shoes so I told my husband. He answered, "Don't tell me. Tell God." So I did. And my heavenly Father gave me a pair of shoes.
     Our first real home was a one-room house in the back yard of one of the saints at our first pastorate. It had been a chicken coop. But I cleaned it and cleaned it and cleaned it . . . and it was home!
     In the summer of 1929 our family arrived in Houston, Texas to

build a church with three buffalo nickels—fifteen cents. Six years later we had a congregation and $65.00 in the building fund. We bought a house and remodeled it into a church. We outgrew that and built a stone church on Palmer Street. When we outgrew Bethel Tabernacle on Palmer Street, we built Greater Bethel Tabernacle on Irvington Street.

Fifteen cents and the blessings of the Lord—it was enough! "God who brought us from a long ways off shall ever be praised."

To God be the glory!

EXIT SISTER FAUSS. REMOVE PHOTO FROM OVERHEAD.

BERTHA: I'm beginning to wonder if I even know how to spell "sacrifice." *(shudders)* Imagine living in a chicken coop!

HILLARY: Oh, it might not be too bad. You are always saying my house is a pigpen.

MAYBELLE: It's interesting.

HILLARY: What? My pigpen?

MAYBELLE: No, this Church family history. Let's dig a little deeper.

BERTHA: The taproot of the Church family runs back to Pentecost, almost two thousand years ago. There are a lot of ancestors and a lot of history between us and the Day of Pentecost.

MAYBELLE: And a lot of suffering and sacrifice . . .

BERTHA: Yes, that, too. *(peers at watch)* We've got time for one more.

PUT PHOTO #7 (W. J. SEYMOUR) ON OVERHEAD.

HILLARY: Who is he?

ENTER JEANNIE SEYMOUR

SIS. SEYMOUR: Why he's my husband . . . W. J. Seymour.

MAYBELLE: Did you hear that, girls? His name is Sey-mour. I wish we could "see more," don't you?

BERTHA: Maybelle, will you be quiet?

SIS. SEYMOUR: Leader of the great Azusa Street revival. You *have* heard of the Azusa Street revival?

HILLARY: Answer her, Bertha. You're the family brain. She's talking to you.

SIS. SEYMOUR: Actually, the revival began in a black janitor's home on Bonnie Brae Street, Los Angeles, April 1906. I, Jeannie Moore, a young single lady, was the first to receive the Holy Ghost with the evidence of speaking in tongues. It was the spark that lit the fire of revival. A few days later Brother Seymour, a young preacher from Houston, received his baptism in the Spirit.

Folks crowded into the little house on Bonnie Brae Street and spilled onto the porch and into the yard. Within a week, we had rented a two-story building, formerly a church, a tenement house and a stable, at 312 Azusa Street. Brother Seymour was the leader . . . if indeed it can be said this revival had a natural leader.

"The news spread far and wide that Los Angeles was being visited with a rushing mighty wind from heaven. The how and why of it [were] found in the very opposite of those conditions that are usually thought necessary for a big revival.

"No instruments of music [were] used. None [were] needed.

"No choir. Bands of angels [were] heard by some in the Spirit and there [was] heavenly singing that [was] inspired by the Holy Ghost.

"No collections [were] taken.

"No bills [were] posted to advertise the meetings.

"No church organization [backed] it.

"All who [were] in touch with God realize[d] as soon as they enter[ed] the meeting that the Holy Ghost [was] the leader. . . . Travelers from afar wend[ed] their way to the headquarters of Azusa Street. There they [found] a two-story whitewashed building. You would hardly expect heavenly visitations there . . . unless you remember[ed] . . . the stable at Bethlehem."[1]

"Food was brought in from day to day for the workers, but no one inquired as to its source. God was recognized as the giver of all, and received ALL the glory and praise."[2]

For three years, seven days a week, from 10:00 in the morning until midnight or later, revival fires burned. Thousands—black, white, Hispanics, Asians, rich and poor, educated and illiterate, found their Pentecost at 312 Azusa Street. Their eyes opened, their vision cleared, they left to carry the gospel around the world.

Many who came to mock, stayed to pray. There was such power in the preached Word, sinners were shaken in their seats. Daily the Lord added to the church and signs and wonders were wrought.

Two years into the revival, Brother Seymour and I were married.

"God could have selected a more impressive person, but He used, rather, this relatively uneducated, obscure gentleman, afflicted with a noticeably defective eye."[2]

He was a humble man of God, with a passionate love for His Savior and deep holiness convictions.

How well do I remember my husband sitting behind two empty shoe boxes, one on top of the other, with his head inside the top one during the service, praying. "there was no pride there."

"In this old building, with its low rafters and bare floors, God took strong men and women to pieces, and put them together again, for His glory. It was a tremendous overhauling process. Pride and self-assertion, self-importance and self-esteem, [could] not survive there."[3]

Over and over I heard Brother Seymour say, "Dear loved ones, these meetings are different from any you ever saw in all your born days. These are Holy Ghost meetings and no flesh can glory in the presence of our God." . . . No flesh can glory in the presence of our God.

To God be the glory . . . forever and ever. Amen.

SONG: "To God Be the Glory"

EXIT JEANNIE SEYMOUR, unless she is leading the song.

EXIT GIRLS

[1]James Tyson, *Chalices of Gold,* 109.
[2]Tyson, 110.
[3]Ewart, *Phenomenon of Pentecost,* 40.

Scene IV

Beholding the Glory

STAGE SETTING: None required

INSTRUCTIONS: Sisters Kilgore, Fauss, and Seymour are seated on the front row with a reverb microphone. After they speak, they step up on the sideline of the stage.

RESPONSIVE READING

The heavens declare the glory of God; and the firmament sheweth his handywork (Psalm 19:1).

Blessed be the LORD God, the God of Israel, who only doeth wondrous things, and blessed be his glorious name for ever: and let the whole earth be filled with his glory (Psalm 72:18-19).

Sing unto the LORD, bless his name; shew forth his salvation from day to day. Declare his glory among the heathen, his wonders among all the people (Psalm 96:2-3).

Arise, shine; for thy light is come, and the glory of the LORD is risen upon thee. For, behold, the darkness shall cover the earth, and gross darkness the people: but the LORD shall arise upon thee, and his glory shall be seen upon thee (Isaiah 60:1-2).

ENTER MAYBELLE, from right, carrying a suitcase in one hand and a book, **Their Story: 20th Century Pentecostals,** *(containing script) in the other. Her nose is in the book. She sets her suitcase down, center stage, and stands reading. Begins sniffing. Pulls out handkerchief and blows nose.*

ENTER BERTHA, from right, wearing glasses and carrying a suitcase.

BERTHA: Hello, Maybelle. May-belle, Hellooooo.

MAYBELLE: *(without looking up, sniffs)* Hi.

BERTHA: Seems like I've said these lines before, but here goes . . . Why in the world are you crying? . . . *(no answer)* Maybelle! Are you lost in another romance?

MAYBELLE: Oh, Bertha, it's so beautiful.

BERTHA: Lines are changing. Last time it was "just so sad." Must be a new book. Are they getting married instead of divorced? *(looks at book cover)* That doesn't look like a Harlequin romance to me.

MAYBELLE: It isn't, but it's a beautiful *love* story. The greatest love story of all. It is the story of a bride and Groom, the Church and Christ.

I got so interested in the Church family roots, I had to know more so I'm reading *Their Story: 20th Century Pentecostals.*

BERTHA: That's an improvement. This research into the Church family tree has shown me some things.

MAYBELLE: Like what?

BERTHA: One thing—the good old days weren't all so "good." And another thing—there were many, many signs and wonders, but there was also *lots* of prayer, fasting, and sacrifice. Where's Hillary?

MAYBELLE: Late as usual. She knows check-out time is 12:00. We'll be the last ones out, as usual.

ENTER HILLARY, from back, carrying a suitcase and waving glasses.

HILLARY: I found them! I found them! *(Stubs her toe and trips.)* Ouch! That hurt! *(Holds toe for a split second, then continues down the aisle, weaving her way through the audience, limping slightly)* Excuse me, please . . . I found them! I found them! . . . *(drops suitcase)* Oops! Could I get through here, please? I'm meeting my sisters in the lobby to check out twenty minutes ago . . . Pardon me. I mean I was supposed to meet them in the lobby twenty minutes ago . . . I found them! I found them! . . . Excuse me, please. Thank you . . . Oh, there you are, girls. Guess what? I found my glasses!

BERTHA: They'd do you more good if you'd wear them.

HILLARY: *(putting on glasses)* You're a fine one to talk about wear . . . Bertha! You're wearing glasses! When did you get glasses?

BERTHA: I've had them for a long time. I finally decided it was ridiculous to stumble around half blind because I was too proud to wear glasses. There were some things at this reunion I wanted to see.

MAYBELLE: Where did you find your glasses, Hillary?

HILLARY: I knew someone would ask that! On my head.

MAYBELLE: On your head? I wonder why I didn't see them.

HILLARY: Because you are half blind, too.

BERTHA: That reminds me, Maybelle. You said that you would have surgery when I wore glasses. I'm wearing glasses.

MAYBELLE: I know, but . . . Hillary, where's your crutches?

HILLARY: I don't need them anymore. My toe wasn't broken.

BERTHA: How do you know?

HILLARY: *(shrugs)* I just know it wasn't. *(looks around)* After I found my glasses, I threw my crutches away and went for a walk around the lake. It's beautiful. You know I had almost forgotten there were leaves on the trees. I stood on the shore and looked—I actually look-ed at the things around me.

MAYBELLE: And?

HILLARY: And I saw things I haven't seen since I was a child. I saw lovely little flowers growing among the rocks. I watched the birds and heard them singing praises to their Creator. I noticed the ripples on the water and the leaves on the trees. I even saw the clouds and took great gulps of fresh air! *(throws arms wide)* It was glorious! The whole earth is filled with the glory of God!

BERTHA: "The heavens declare the glory of God; and the firmament sheweth his handywork." I wonder how long it has been since I went outside at night, gazed into the heavens, counted the stars, and reflected on the glory of God. . . . Too long. I think I'll do that tonight.

HILLARY: Me, too. What about you, Maybelle?

MAYBELLE: The only lights I see at night are headlights and street lights with rainbows around them. You know, I'm getting rather weary of rainbows!

HILLARY: *(looks at audience)* I had almost forgotten there were other people in the world. I was so nearsighted about the only person I saw was ME.

BERTHA: I was so farsighted I couldn't see the things right under my nose. With my vision corrected, I see treasures I hadn't noticed before because they were too close to me.

MAYBELLE: Treasures? Like what?

BERTHA: Like the precious heritage that has been handed down to our Church family by our ancestors. Treasures that have been preserved through much sacrifice and suffering. Things like the privilege to pray, the joy of worship, the beauty of holiness . . .

MAYBELLE: I still don't see any beauty in holiness. We're living in a different age than Sister Kilgore and Sister Fauss. It's not important . . .

BERTHA: Maybelle, look around you. Don't you see the glory of God shining on the faces of these beautiful, godly ladies?

MAYBELLE: *(sadly)* No, I just see a sea of blurry faces.

BERTHA: Oh, Maybelle, *please,* get your vision corrected. You are missing seeing the glorious works of God. I see the glory of God reflected all over this congregation. *(Points out ladies with glowing countenances)* Look at that lady . . . and that lady . . . and that lady.

MAYBELLE: *(sobs)* I really would like to see the glory of God, but I can't. I want my vision corrected, but I . . . I . . . I'm scared. I talk a lot about love, but deep down . . . I guess it's a cover-up. Oh, girls, what if I have surgery, and I see myself as I really am?

BERTHA: You will—when your vision is corrected. When I put on my glasses, I saw myself. It wasn't a pretty sight. I saw pride and self-righteousness . . . filthy rags! And I hate filth! Then I heard Sister Seymour.

SISTER SEYMOUR: No flesh can glory in His presence. No flesh can glory in His presence.

BERTHA: Oh, girls, let me assure you it was worth humbling myself to see the Lord "high and lifted up."

HILLARY: I saw selfishness and deceit in me. I saw someone who wanted to be center stage all the time. I wanted all the glory. I was a lot of fluff and puff! Then I heard Sister Fauss.

SISTER FAUSS: To God be the glory. To God be the glory!

HILLARY: Suddenly I realized I would never see the glory of God until I gave Him the glory! The glory belongs to the King, ladies! The glory belongs to the King!

MAYBELLE: But surgery means I will have to make adjustments in my lifestyle. I'll have to align my priorities, my convictions, my standards with God's. It may mean some sacrifices . . . sacrifices and suffering . . . but I hear Sister Kilgore.

SISTER KILGORE: For our light affliction, which is but for a moment, worketh for us a far more exceeding and eternal weight of glory.

BERTHA: When you surrender, Maybelle, you will see the glory of God in the beauty of holiness—because God's glory and His holiness are inseparable. His glory and His holiness are inseparable!

MAYBELLE: I'll do it! I'll do it! I do so desperately want to see the glory of God.

HILLARY: Look, Bertha. I see it! I see the glory of the Lord in the sanctuary. I see it!

SISTER KILGORE, SISTER FAUSS AND SISTER SEYMOUR move quickly to center stage. All join hands and raise them heavenward.

BERTHA: "ARISE, SHINE [Ladies]; for thy light is come, and the glory of the LORD is risen upon thee."

ALL: TO GOD BE THE GLORY FOREVER AND EVER . . . AMEN.

SONG: "Majesty" (by congregation)

2

Role Play

CAST:
  Man's voice
  Recording Angel (A)
  Guardian Angel (B)
  Lisa Marie (wife and mother)
  Rhonda Renae (musician)
  Linda Jo (encourager)
  Donna June (intercessor)
  Vicki Lynn (teacher)

Let's Play Like

Stage I, Scene I

PROPS:
  tape of man's voice
  tape recorder
  large book
  large feather pen, type used in weddings
  miscellaneous items carried by girls

MAN'S VOICE: *(taped using mike with echo effect)* "Unto the church of God which is at" *(place of program)*, "to them that are sanctified in Christ Jesus, called to be saints . . ." came the word of the Lord saying, *Before I formed thee in the belly I knew thee; and before thou camest forth out of the womb I sanctified thee, and I ordained thee [as saints in the world]* (based on I Corinthians 1:2; Jeremiah 1:4-5).

ENTER ANGELS. Recording angel (A) is carrying a large black book (containing a copy of the script). She puts it down and starts flipping through the pages.

131

ANGEL B: And what are you recording today?

ANGEL A: The names of the little ones and the Father's plan for their lives.

ANGEL B: *(looks over A's shoulder and reads from script as A writes)* Linda Jo, called to be an encourager. *(rolls eyes upward)* Oh, Lord, please don't assign me as her guardian angel.

ANGEL A: Why not? Encouragers are nice people.

ANGEL B: Oh, I know that. It's the people they associate with that's the problem. I was assigned to an encourager once and there was always someone crying on her shoulder . . . always! It was enough to depress even an angel. *(reads)* Lisa Marie, called to be a wife and mother. Is that all?

ANGEL A: *(looks up)* Is what all?

ANGEL B: Is that all the Father expects Lisa Marie to do with her life, just be a wife and mother?

ANGEL A: Have you ever been a wife and mother?

ANGEL B: Welllll, no.

ANGEL A: I thought not or you wouldn't ask such a foolish question. *(writes again)*

ANGEL B: Rhonda Renae, called to be a musician. Ohhhh, I hope our Father appoints me as her guardian angel. I love music. When will Rhonda Renae's angel be assigned to her?

ANGEL A: *(scratches head with pen)* In about nine months, earth time. Right now her mother's angel is standing guard. In fact, all the little ones I am recording today are still under the care of their mother's angel.

ANGEL B: When you finish here, let's go over to Security so I can sign up for Rhonda Renae. Musicians are terribly popular with guardian angels. As soon as word gets out that one is going to be born, there'll be a waiting list for her. *(reads, as Angel A writes)* Vicki Lynn, called to be a teacher. Teacher, now that word covers a multitude of roles. Guarding a teacher of adults I can handle, although sometimes it's a bit boring . . . but a teen teacher. Oh, Lord, deliver me. Have you ever had your wings clipped by a paper airplane?

ANGEL A: Can't say that I have. I'm in Accounting, not Security. *(writes again)*

ANGEL B: *(reads)* Sarah Beth, called to be a missionary. Oooohhh, I just changed my mind. I want to guard Sarah Beth. Missionaries lead such exciting lives.

ANGEL A: I would think following a missionary around would be extremely tiring. Think of deputation!

ANGEL B: Dep-u-ta-tion? Oh . . . I'd forgotten about deputation. Maybe I'll ask for Rhonda Renae after all. Although beginning musicians can be awfully hard on the ears . . . and nerves!

ANGEL A: One more entry and I'm finished for today. *(writes)* Donna June, called to be an intercessor.

ANGEL B: Uh-oh, she may not like that.

ANGEL A: Why not?

ANGEL B: Well, for one thing, it's hard work. And for another thing, there's not much glory to it. It's all done behind the scenes, you know. There's no spotlight or applause for the intercessor.

ANGEL A: Well, someone has to do it. And besides, I can't change Donna June's calling. I'm just the recording angel. The heavenly Father assigns the roles.

ANGEL B: If Donna June fills that role, she'll need two angels.

ANGEL A: Two? Why?

ANGEL B: Have you ever been guardian angel to an intercessor?

ANGEL A: Of course not. Like I told you, I'm not in the Security Department, I'm in Accounting. So of course I've never been a guardian angel to an intercessor. *(closes book)*

ANGEL B: I thought not, or you wouldn't ask such a foolish question. Intercessors need a battalion of angels because they fight great battles. Now I think I'll go sign up for Rhonda Renae. Like I said, musicians are so popular. If I don't get my bid in early, I don't stand a chance of being assigned to her, and nine months earth time isn't long up here.

ANGEL A: You're right about that. Time doesn't mean much in eternity. I'll go with you.

EXIT ANGELS

Scene II

ENTER GIRLS, dressed like little girls (four or five years old), bows in hair, tennis shoes, anklets, etc.

LISA MARIE carries a doll wrapped in a blanket.

VICKI LYNN carries coloring books and crayons and has large pencil stuck in her hair.

RHONDA RENAE has a child's keyboard and snaps fingers as she walks as if hearing music and keeping a beat.

LINDA JO carries a jump rope and occasionally jumps.

LISA MARIE: Let's play like I'm the mother and you all are the kids.

VICKI LYNN: No, I'd rather play school. I'll be the teacher. You all be the students.

RHONDA RENAE: But I want to play church, and I'll be the piano player. You all can be whatever you want to be. *(plunks "I Drop My Dolly in the Dirt" on keyboard)*

VICKI LYNN: Don't be silly, Rhonda Renae. We can't sing "I Drop My Dolly" in church.

RHONDA RENAE: I didn't drop my dolly in church, Vicki Lynn. I dropped her in the dirt. *(sings and plays)* I dropped my dolly in the dirt. I ask my dolly if it hurt, but all my dolly could say . . .

LINDA JO: *(claps)* That was good, Rhonda Renae. Someday you'll be a great pianist. I just know it. What else can you play?

RHONDA RENAE: *(proudly)* I can play, "Mary Had a Little Lamb." *(does so)*

VICKI LYNN: You can't sing that in church either. We'll have to play school and I'll be the teacher.

RHONDA RENAE: But I want to play church.

LISA MARIE: And I want to play house and be the mother.

LINDA JO: *(scratches head)* Now, let's see . . . I know what. Let's play church.

RHONDA RENAE: That's what I said.

LISA MARIE: But I want to be the mother.

VICKI LYNN: If I can't be the teacher, I'm going home. *(starts to leave)*

LINDA JO: *(yells louder)* Let's play church and Lisa Marie can be the mother who brings her children to Sunday school.

LISA MARIE: Okay. Where's the nursery? I'll stay in there and visit with my friends.

LINDA JO: And Vicki Lynn can play like she's the teacher . . .

VICKI LYNN: Oh, that's a good idea, Linda Jo. *(haughtily)* I'll teach all you little kids. . .

LISA MARIE: You won't teach me, I'll be in the nursery.

VICKI LYNN: But we can't sing, "Mary Had a Little Lamb."

LINDA JO: I know that, Vicki Lynn. *(scratches head)* Now let's see. . . Oh, I've got it. I know a song we can sing that sounds just like "Mary Had a Little Lamb." *(sings and RHONDA RENAE plunks along on keyboard)* "Let's all go to Sunday school, Sunday school, Sunday school. Let's all go to Sunday school and learn the Golden Rule."

ENTER DONNA JUNE, chewing bubble gum and blowing bubbles.

GIRLS: Hi, Donna June.

DONNA JUNE: What are you all playing?

LINDA JO: Do you want to play with us?

DONNA JUNE: *(blows bubble)* I'm not sure. It all depends on what you are playing. I can't play anything rough. *(blows bubble)* Let's have a bubble blowing contest.

LINDA JO: Blow another bubble, Donna June. You're a good bubble blower.

DONNA JUNE makes a production of blowing two or three bubbles with LINDA JO encouraging her.

VICKI LYNN: We're going to play church, Donna June. And you can't chew gum in church. If you don't want to play, that's fine with us. I'm the teacher, and Lisa Marie is the mother who brings her children to church, and Rhonda Renae is the piano player and—

DONNA JUNE: What can I be?

VICKI LYNN: Hummmmm . . . I guess you can be the pray-er.

DONNA JUNE: The pray-er? You mean the one who goes to the prayer room before church and stays late and prays in the altar while everyone else goes for pizza?

VICKY LYNN: Yep. Every church has to have one or two pray-ers.

DONNA JUNE: But I don't want to be a pray-er. I'd rather be a player.

VICKI LYNN: You can't. Rhonda Renae is the piano player.

DONNA JUNE: Then I'll play the organ.

LISA MARIE: Linda Jo, what are you going to be?

LINDA JO: *(shrugs)* I don't know . . .

VICKI LYNN: I know. You can be the pastor's wife who tells the preacher when he does something wrong.

DONNA JUNE: That's what I want to be—the preacher's wife who wears a new dress and sits on the front row.

VICKI LYNN: Sorry, that's Linda Jo's part.

LINDA JO: That's okay. Let Donna June be the preacher's wife. I don't want to be anybody important. I'll just be the saint who sits in the pew and hollers "Amen" and gives in the offering and cleans the church and sells peanut brittle and brings people to church and prays in the altar and the prayer room and—

VICKI LYNN: Okay. Okay. It's not much fun just being a saint, but someone has to do it. Let's go play on my patio. Donna June, you have to spit out your gum!

GIRLS start to EXIT.

LISA MARIE: *(on the way out)* I just thought of something. We don't have a preacher. Who's going to be the preacher?

VICKI LYNN: Don't worry about that. We'll have song service and Sunday school class. Then we'll have one of those good services where the Spirit moves and we don't have any preaching. We don't need a preacher.

EXIT GIRLS

In Real Life

Stage II, Scene I

PROPS
    tape (man's voice)
    tape recorder
    large book

large pen
giant bandaid
2 telephones and small tables (on opposite sides of stage)

INSTRUCTIONS: Angel B's elbow should be colored to resemble an injury.

MAN'S VOICE: *(taped with mike on echo effect)* And I sought for [someone] among them, that should make up the hedge, and stand in the gap before me for the land, that I should not destroy it (based on Ezekiel 22:30).

ENTER ANGELS. ANGEL A carrying pen and book containing script.

ANGEL B: *(wings drooping, halo askew)* Boy, I am worn out, totally exhausted, dead on my feet, beat! . . .

ANGEL A: You are also talking like a human being.

ANGEL B: Sometimes I feel more human than angelic. I don't know where the idea got started that angels are tireless. I am more than ready for Rest and Recreation. I'll tell you, I was about ready to resign when—

ANGEL A: Resign? Now you *are* talking like a human being.

ANGEL B: *(sighs)* I know. I think humans are a bad influence on us angels. Anyway, the Father finally sent a substitute to relieve me. In fact, He sent four angels to take my place.

ANGEL A: Four? Why four? Did Rhonda Renae join a rock band?

ANGEL B: Rhonda Renae? Who's Rhonda Renae? Oh, I remember. She's the musician I signed up to guard. I didn't get that assignment.

ANGEL A: Then let me guess. You got Linda Jo, the encourager.

ANGEL B: No, it's worse than that. Guess again.

ANGEL A: Donna June, the intercessor?

ANGEL B: Donna June, the intercessor? That's a laugh. Apparently, you don't know Donna June. Haven't you been paying attention to the events on earth? I warned you about Donna June's assignment.

ANGEL A: And I told you that I only record the roles, I don't assign them.

ANGEL B: Things don't always turn out the way the heavenly Father plans them, you know. There's a little thing called "the human will" that often gets in the way. I think your books are outdated.

ANGEL A: *(sighs)* I know. It's so hard to keep up with the fast-paced human race. I'm getting ready to bring my books up to date now. *(flips page)* Let's see, looks like the last entry was made about thirty years ago. The girls were about five years old then. So you weren't assigned to Donna June?

ANGEL B: No, I didn't get Donna June. Thank the Lord! Guess again.

ANGEL A: I'm tired of guessing. Tell me.

ANGEL B: I was assigned to Lisa Marie.

ANGEL A: Lisa Marie? Oh, Lisa Marie, the wife and mother. Well, that should have been a snap.

ANGEL B: A snap? Are you kidding? . . . and I do mean "kid-ing." She had three kids. And that's not the half of it. They weren't just kids. They were boys! Every time she got pregnant I prayed for a girl! I had just adjusted to guarding one boy, then there was another boy, and then another boy! There was a four-year-old, a two-year-old, and a baby. Then the boys were six, four, and two. There were boys all over the place! It looked like a dozen. Now they are fourteen, twelve, and ten. The youngest just got his first skateboard. The middle one just got his first paper route, and the oldest just got his first motorcycle. And I'm about to have my first nervous breakdown!

ANGEL A: So that's why the Father sent four angels to replace you. Well, it could have been worse.

ANGEL B: Worse? I don't see how. I've dug boys out of trash dumpsters, hung on to shirttails to keep them from falling into alligator pits, stood between them and pit bulls. Look at my elbow! (shows "injured" elbow) Just look! This was the last straw. I'll tell you nothing—and I mean *nothing*—moves as fast as a ten-year-old on a skateboard! Just as I reached for him, he flipped. I got this and he broke his arm! I really felt bad about that, but even angels have limits!

ANGEL A: Oh, you poor thing. Here let me fix it for you. *(puts Band-Aid on angel's elbow)* But you could have been assigned to the intercessor and had to fight demons.

ANGEL B: *(slaps forehead)* The intercessor! The rest of the story is—I got in on that, too.

ANGEL A: What are you talking about?

ANGEL B: There's nothing like boys to make an intercessor out of their mother! I wish now I'd signed up for Sarah Beth.

ANGEL A: Sarah Beth?

ANGEL B: Yes, Sarah Beth. You know, the missionary.

ANGEL A: The missiona . . . Oh, you didn't hear about her?

ANGEL B: No. What about her?

ANGEL A: *(flips pages)* Look. Read it for yourself.

ANGEL B: *(reads slowly with voice rising in horror)* Sarah Beth, called to be a saint and a missionary . . . aborted. Aborted? ABORTED! Sarah Beth was aborted?

ANGEL A: *(nods slowly)* Yes.

SONG: *"What Was I Supposed to Be?"* (optional)

ANGEL B: Ohhhhhh, that's so sad . . . I thought . . . I thought her mother's angel was standing guard.

ANGEL A: She was. But remember mankind's right of choice can supercede even the Father's will. The angel could not save the baby. I've never seen an angel so angry. She wanted to resign . . . to leave the mother unguarded.

ANGEL B: Well, I should think so. That woman doesn't deserve a guardian angel.

ANGEL A: But the heavenly Father said no.

ANGEL B: No? You mean Sarah's mother is still under the Father's care?

ANGEL A: Yes. The love of the Father never ceases to amaze me.

ANGEL B: But what about the mission field where Sarah Beth had been ordained to go? What about the lost in that country?

ANGEL A: I understand the Father is looking for someone to make up the hedge and stand in the gap.

ANGEL B: Don't tell Lisa Marie.

ANGEL A: Why not?

ANGEL B: She'd do it! And she's already standing in one gap. She's stretched about as far as she can stretch.

ANGEL A: What are you talking about?

ANGEL B: Look. Why don't you bring your records up to date and then you'll know what I'm talking about. *(yawns)* Meanwhile, I'm going to take a nap. See you around. *(starts to leave, calls over shoulder)* You might start with Donna June.

EXIT ANGEL B

ANGEL A: *(shakes head at departing friend)* I don't see how three boys can wear an angel completely out. *(flips pages)* Donna June . . . A . . . B . . . C . . . D *(starts to EXIT, reading as she goes)* Here she is . . . Donna June, called to be an intercessor.

EXIT ANGEL A

Scene II

ENTER DONNA JUNE, dressed in an old robe, hair tied in a scarf, chewing gum, blowing bubbles, drags to the telephone and dials.

SOUND: TELEPHONE RINGING

ENTER LINDA JO, on opposite side of stage, answers the telephone.

LINDA JO: *(scratches head)* Well, let's see . . . I wonder who is calling at this hour of the morning. I hope it's not another emergency. *(picks up phone)* Hello . . .

DONNA JUNE: Linda Jo . . . I mean Sister Short, this is Donna June.

LINDA JO: Good morning, Sister Donna. How are you?

DONNA JUNE: I thought you'd never ask. No one ever does. I have one of my terrible headaches. I missed Bible study and not one person has called to see about me . . . not even your husba . . . I mean, not even the Pastor . . . I mean, no one.

LINDA JO: Why, Sister Donna, it's only 8:15. Brother Short was up late last night at the hospital. Sister Lisa's youngest boy was playing on his skateboard in their driveway after church last night and broke his arm.

DONNA JUNE: I'm so afraid one of my children is going to get hurt. There is no way I'd let them have a skateboard.

LINDA JO: *(sighs)* I know. I was going to call you later. I wanted to give you time to get your children off to school.

DONNA JUNE: The children had to get themselves off to school. I just pulled myself out of bed to ask you to call Lisa Marie and ask her to pray for me. I've got lots of confidence in her prayers.

LINDA JO: What's the problem, Donna June?

DONNA JUNE: My head is just killing me.

LINDA JO: That's too bad. Any time you are sick, Sister Donna June, just call. We'll be happy to come and pray for you.

DONNA JUNE: Why do I always have to do the calling? Why don't you . . . I mean, why doesn't someone call me? You know how sick . . . I mean, everyone knows what poor health I'm in.

LINDA JO: As soon as Brother Short gets a minute, we'll run by. . . .

DONNA JUNE: No, don't bother. I know how busy you are. Everyone is busy . . . too busy to bother with me. Just because we can't afford to pay our tithes and can't make it to every service . . . No one understands how poor and sick I really am.

LINDA JO: I'm sorry you missed the service last night. We had a missionary. The service was outstanding. The Spirit of the Lord moved and—

DONNA JUNE: I do wish someone had told me that a missionary was coming.

LINDA JO: It was announced twice Sunday.

DONNA JUNE: Sunday? Oh, well, we were out of town. *(Husband)* bought a new boat, you know, and the only time we have to go to the lake is the weekend.

LINDA JO: *(scratches head)* Oh, I see. Anyway, the Spirit of the Lord moved in a wonderful way and—

DONNA JUNE: I do so love missionary slides. It almost like going to the movi . . . I mean, they are so moving. I'm sure the Lord would have called me to the mission field if I had been blessed with better health. But I guess it's just as well, He didn't. *(Husband)* isn't the least bit interested in missions—not even in the slides! And I can't stand bugs! *(shivers)*

LINDA JO: We didn't have slides last night. Just a wonderful move of the Holy Ghost.

DONNA JUNE: If I had come, I couldn't have stayed. My headache started about 8:30 and I declare I didn't sleep a wink all night.

LINDA JO: *(scratches head)* Well, now let's see . . . Your headache started at 8:30. Church started at 7:30.

DONNA JUNE: I know what time church starts!

LINDA JO: Do you? The Spirit of the Lord moved mightily upon us all. When the missionary told about going through a country on his way home where there was not a missionary, a spirit of intercession swept over the congregation. It was as if the Holy Ghost was grieving through us.

DONNA JUNE: My, my, that wouldn't have been good for my head at all!

LINDA JO: Anyway, I feel led to have ladies' prayer meeting every morning next week to pray especially for missions.

DONNA JUNE: Ladies' prayer meeting? Next week? Every morning?

LINDA JO: Yes, every morning at 9:00. I'll be happy to come by for you Monday morning.

DONNA JUNE: Monday morning? Oh . . . ahhhh . . . oh . . . ahhhhh . . . Monday morning? It seems like I have something . . . Oh, yes, how could I forget? I have a doctor's appointment Monday at 11:30 so I just couldn't possibly make it to prayer meeting.

LINDA JO: Well, how about Tuesday?

DONNA JUNE: Tuesday? . . . Ooooohhhh . . . ahhhhhh . . . Tuesday? Oh, yes, Tuesday I have an appointment with my hairdresser.

LINDA JO: Oh, I see. Well, if you decide you want to come any day next week, just call. I'll be glad to come by and pick you up.

DONNA JUNE: I will. Say, I just remembered this is the day they are having a four-family garage sale in the next block. I've got to hurry or all the bargains will be gone. I'll call you if I feel like going to prayer meeting. Goodbye. Oh, Sister Short, don't forget to call Lisa Marie and ask her to pray for me. And you and Brother Short don't need to bother to come by. I won't be home.

DONNA JUNE hangs up the phone and EXITS.

LINDA JO: *(hangs up phone, scratches head)* Well, let's see. Whom shall I call first? Vicki Lynn . . . here's her number. *(picks up phone and dials)*

SOUND: TELEPHONE RINGING

ENTER VICKI LYNN, dressed for work and carrying purse, answers phone used by Donna.

VICKI LYNN: Hello.

LINDA JO: Good morning, Sister Vicki. This is Sister Short. How are you this morning?

VICKI LYNN: In a hurry as usual.

LINDA JO: Well this won't take but a minute. Last night in the service I felt—

VICKI LYNN: *(digs in purse, pulls out car keys and swings them impatiently as she talks)* Oh, wasn't that a wonderful service?

LINDA JO: It certainly was. I feel deeply impressed that we need to do more for missions.

VICKI LYNN: Oh, I do too. In fact, *(husband)* and I were so moved last night, we gave an extra dollar in the offering.

LINDA JO: You did? Oh, that's great . . . I guess. I want us to have ladies' prayer meeting—

VICKI LYNN: Ladies' prayer meeting?

LINDA JO: Yes, every morning next week at 9:00.

VICKI LYNN: Every morning? But, Sister Short, you know how busy I am. Besides my part-time job teaching school, I am involved in every area of the church. In fact, I'm more than involved . . . I am in charge of most of them. *(counts off on fingers)* I teach a Sunday school class. I am secretary of the Ladies Auxiliary. I sing at the nursing home. I am a sponsor of the youth. I—

LINDA JO: I know, Sister Vicki. That's why I called you. I was sure you would want to be involved in prayer meeting too.

VICKI LYNN: Oh, I do want to. But I don't see how I can squeeze another thing into my schedule. Sometimes I feel like *(husband)* and I are carrying the whole load. We did keep this church going when we didn't have a pastor, you know. But you wouldn't remember that.

LINDA JO: *(aside)* I'm not likely to forget it.

VICKI LYNN: *(continues nonstop)* You and Brother Short were off at Bible school having a good time. If it hadn't been for *(husband)* and me this church would have gone down the drain long ago.

LINDA JO: Brother Short and I do appreciate you and your husband, Sister Vicki. Now about the prayer meeting—I'm sure you realize that the most important role we can fill in the church is that of intercessor.

VICKI LYNN: *(wrinkles brow)* Intercessor? Intercessor? Oh, you mean, in prayer. Well, Sister Short, I do pray. I pray off and on all day—when I'm off the phone and on the go. And like I said, I have filled about every role there is in the church—except pastor—and I guess I could do that if I needed to. But I just simply cannot make time for prayer meeting. There comes a time when a person has to say no. Why don't you call some of the older ladies . . . you know, the ones who don't have anything else to do? I'm just too busy—

LINDA JO: *(scratches head)* So I see. So I see. And I agree, you are much too busy.

VICKI LYNN: I hate to cut this short, Sister Short, but I'm going to be late for my exercise class if I don't hurry. I'll see you Saturday night at the spaghetti supper. *(hangs up)*

EXIT VICKI LYNN

LINDA JO: *(hangs up phone, sighs deeply)* Well, let's see who's next on the list . . . Rhonda Renae. *(picks up phone and dials)*

SOUND: TELEPHONE RINGING

ENTER RHONDA RENAE, snapping fingers, swinging hips and singing.

RHONDA RENAE: *(answers phone in sing song voice)* Hel-loooo.

LINDA JO: Good morning, Sister Rhonda. This is Sister Short. Didn't we have a wonderful service last night?

RHONDA RENAE: Oh, yes. The music was simply heavenly.

LINDA JO: And the sermon was outstanding.

RHONDA RENAE: Sermon? Oh, yes, the missionary did have a delightful voice.

LINDA JO: I felt deeply impressed that we should do more for missions, so I am calling for ladies' prayer meeting every morning next week at 9:00.

RHONDA RENAE: Ladies' prayer meeting? Every morning?

LINDA JO: Yes. We need to intercede for the lost.

RHONDA RENAE: Well, that's a good idea, Sister Short. There are so many ladies in our church who don't do anything.

LINDA JO: Then I can count on you being there?

RHONDA RENAE: Me? That's not what I said. I have all I can do as head of the music department. My talent is music, not prayer.

LINDA JO: But, Sister Rhonda, prayer is not a talent. We are all called to prayer.

RHONDA RENAE: Oh, I pray. I pray every day . . . well, almost every day. Besides I consider my music my prayer. I offer up praise and worship when I sing and play.

LINDA JO: That's true. But there is another type of prayer, called intercession. . . .

RHONDA RENAE: Yes, but that's not my calling. I'm filling my role and I simply can't take on another.

LINDA JO: I see . . . well, I'll let you go.

RHONDA RENAE: Thanks for calling. I always like to know what is going on in the other departments, even if I can't help. Goodbye. Oh, wait a minute, Sister Short. Do you need me to play for your prayer meetings?

LINDA JO: No, thank you, Sister Rhonda. We're not going to have music, just prayer. Goodbye. *(hangs up)*

RHONDA RENAE: *(hangs up)* No music? Just prayer? I wonder what kind of a service that will be?

EXIT RHONDA RENAE

LINDA JO: *(scratches head)* Well, let's see. Oh, yes, Donna June wanted me to ask Lisa Marie to pray for her. I wonder if Donna June ever prays for herself? *(picks up phone and dials)*

SOUND: TELEPHONE RINGING

ENTER LISA MARIE, putting on apron, as she answers the phone.

LISA MARIE: Hello.

LINDA JO: Sister Lisa Marie, this is Sister Short.

LISA MARIE: Oh, Sister Short, would you tell your husband again how much we appreciate him staying with us at the hospital last night?

LINDA JO: I'll be glad to. How is Brian's arm?

LISA MARIE: Seems to be doing fine. He's still asleep. That pain medicine knocked him out.

LINDA JO: Before I forget, Donna June asked me to ask you to pray for her. She has one of her headaches this morning. I don't know why she didn't call you herself.

LISA MARIE: I'll be glad to pray for her. I was just getting ready to have my prayer time when you called.

LINDA JO: Last night in the service I felt strongly impressed that we should have a ladies' prayer meeting every morning next week.

LISA MARIE: Ladies' prayer meeting? Every morning?

LINDA JO: *(sighs heavily)* I know everyone is busy. It's so hard to find a time that is convenient for everyone.

LISA MARIE: Oh, Sister Short . . .

LINDA JO: I'll understand if you can't come. I know you have your hands full with three boys and one of them with a broken arm and—

LISA MARIE: But, Sister Short—

LINDA JO: Don't worry about it, Sister Lisa. It was a good idea and I really felt like it was the Lord's will, but if no one can come, I guess—

LISA MARIE: No one can come? But, Sister Short, I can come. I think it's a wonderful idea.

LINDA JO: Wonderful? You think it's wonderful?

LISA MARIE: Oh, yes. Lately, I've felt such a spirit of travail and intercession during my prayer time. I didn't understand my burden until last night. As the missionary spoke, the Lord showed me that the Spirit had been praying through me for missions. I'm so glad we'll be having prayer meetings. There seems to be more power when we agree together.

LINDA JO: Then I can count on you to be there?

LISA MARIE: Of course, you can count on me.

LINDA JO: Oh, thank you, Sister Lisa Marie. Thank you. Thank you! Now I'll let you go. Goodbye and God bless. *(hangs up phone)* And thank You, God, for the Lisa Maries. . . . Thank You!

LISA MARIE: *(hangs up phone, shakes head)* I wonder why Sister Short was so grateful? Just her nature, I guess.

EXIT BOTH

The Last Act

Stage III

PROPS
>   tape
>   tape recorder
>   large book
>   large pen
>   school bell
>   magazines

chairs, at least one rocking chair, plants, table, lamp, etc. *(for sitting room scene)*

sewing bag (knitting or crocheting)

INSTRUCTIONS: GIRLS are dressed as old ladies, using canes, walkers, etc.

ANGEL A speaks from behind the scene, using a vibrato mike with echo effect. She interrupts the girls' conversation, calling them out. Only the one called hears the angel's voice and only Rhonda Renae hears the heavenly music.

MAN'S VOICE: *(taped with mike on echo) For what is your life? It is even a vapour, that appeareth for a little time, and then vanisheth away* (James 4:14).

ENTER LISA MARIE, hobbles in, sits down, pulls out knitting or crocheting.

ENTER LINDA JO, hobbles in, looks all around.

LINDA JO: *(scratches head)* Now let's see . . . did I just come in or am I going out?

LISA MARIE: *(wrinkles brow)* I'm not sure . . . but I think . . . you came in.

LINDA JO: Oh, good, then I can sit down. *(does so, scratches head)* Well, now let's see . . . where are we?

LISA MARIE: *(smiles)* I don't remember, but isn't it nice that we're here together?

LINDA JO: It's wonderful. You know we've been friends for a long time.

LISA MARIE: Yes, a long, long time. In fact, about all our lives.

LINDA JO: I remember when we used to play church together.

LISA MARIE: Yes, and you were the saint. You've always been a saint.

LINDA JO: And you were the mother. You loved being a mother.

LISA MARIE: I still do. Yes, we've been friends for a long, long time. You always have been my best friend, but there's one thing I can't remember.

LINDA JO: What's that?

LISA MARIE: What's your name?

LINDA JO: My name? *(scratches head)* Well, let's see . . . uhhhhhh . . . my name? Uhhhhh . . . do you have to know right now?

ENTER DONNA JUNE, hobbling and grumbling. LINDA JO mutters and mumbles to herself, trying to remember her name.

DONNA JUNE: Linda Jo, I do declare to my time, you've got my chair again!

LINDA JO: Oh, thank you. *(loudly, aside to Lisa Marie)* It's Linda Jo.

LISA MARIE: That's right. Now I remember.

DONNA JUNE: Thank you? What in the world are you thanking me for? Linda Jo, you know I can't sit in those other chairs. They're hard on my back. Now get up and let me have my chair.

LINDA JO staggers to her feet. DONNA JUNE plops down in her chair.

DONNA JUNE: I don't know what you've got to smile about, Lisa Marie.

LISA MARIE: I don't know what you've got to frown about, Donna June.

DONNA JUNE: You don't know? I've told you a hundred times. I've got arthritis, rheumatism, neuritis, hepat—

LINDA JO: It's so nice being here together. Just like old times. We've got a lot to be thankful for, girls.

DONNA JUNE: A lot to be thankful for? Ha! Stiff knees, cataracts, false teeth. Why I can't even chew gum anymore.

ENTER RHONDA RENAE and VICKI LYNN, helping one another, stumbling, making quite a scene. RHONDA RENAE is singing. Eventually, they find their chairs and sit down.

LISA MARIE: Good morning, girls. Did you sleep well?

VICKI LYNN: As well as can be expected considerin' Rhonda Renae snored all night long. It's a good thing she's about half deaf or she'd never get any sleep. She'd keep herself awake all night.

DONNA JUNE: Well, I didn't sleep a wink myself all night.

VICKI LYNN: What's the matter, Donna June? Can't you get your lumps to fit the mattress?

RHONDA RENAE: *(yells)* What's the matter with this rocking chair? I can't get it started.

DONNA JUNE: It's not the rocker. It's you.

RHONDA RENAE: Heh? Did you say I'm off my rocker?

DONNA JUNE: *(shakes head vigorously)* No, but it's a thought.

SOUND: SCHOOL BELL

ANGEL A: *(behind scene on echo mike)* Vicky Lynn . . .

VICKI LYNN looks up and around.

DONNA JUNE: *(continues nonstop)* Thank God, there's nothing wrong with my mind; it's my poor body that's so afflicted. I was sure you could hear me groaning last night, Lisa Marie. Why didn't you come and pray for me? You know how much I depend upon your prayers.

LISA MARIE: I did pray for you, Donna June.

RHONDA RENAE: *(yells)* Do you ever pray for yourself, Donna June?

DONNA JUNE: It's a funny thing to me you never hear what I say to you, but you always hear when I'm talking to someone else.

SOUND: SCHOOL BELL

ANGEL A: Vicki Lynn . . . called to be a teacher.

VICKI LYNN gets to feet and staggers to the front of the stage.

LINDA JO: Now, girls, let's don't spoil this beautiful day a quarrelin'. Remember how much fun we used to have? . . .

GIRLS ad-lib conversation which fades out. They continue to pantomine in background as attention shifts to Vicki Lynn.

VICKI LYNN: I hear the dismissal bell. Someone is calling my name. *(louder)* Yes? Did You call me?

ANGEL A: Vicki Lynn, it's time to come home.

VICKI LYNN: *(face brightening)* Oh, school must be dismissed. Good-bye, girls, it's been fun playing with you, but I've got to go home now. My Father is calling me.

VICKI LYNN EXITS unnoticed by others.

LINDA JO: *(fades in)* . . . how we used to play church together. Lisa Marie was the mother.

DONNA JUNE: I was the pastor's wife.

LINDA JO: Yes, Rhonda Renae was the pianist and Vicki Lynn was the tea— *(looks around)* Where's Vicki Lynn?

GIRLS look around in shock.

LISA MARIE: She's not here. She's gone.

GIRLS: Gone? Vicki Lynn is gone?

LISA MARIE: Yes. She's gone.

DONNA JUNE: *(slowly in amazement)* Well . . . I always thought I'd be the first one to go . . . as sickly as I am.

RHONDA RENAE: Heh? What did you say, Donna June?

DONNA JUNE: *(yells)* I said I always thought I'd be the first one to go as sickly as I am.

RHONDA RENAE: Bah! You're always goin' on 'bout how sick you are. Why, if you were as sick as you say you are, you'd'a died a long time ago. You mark my word, you'll be the last one of us to go.

DONNA JUNE: I will not!

RHONDA RENAE: Ahhhhh, you will too.

DONNA JUNE: I most certainly will not.

RHONDA RENAE: Will too!

DONNA JUNE: Will not.

RHONDA RENAE: Yes, you will.

DONNA JUNE: No, I will not.

LINDA JO: *(yells)* Girls! Quit your fussing. What are you fussin' about anyway?

DONNA JUNE: Rhonda Renae said I would . . . uhhhhhh. . . . She said I would . . . uhhhhhh, I would . . . Well, whatever she said I would do, I will not do it!

RHONDA RENAE: If I said she'd do it, she will.

LINDA JO: Do what?

RHONDA RENAE: Uhhhhh . . . uhhhhhh . . . oh, never mind.

LINDA JO: Please, girls, don't fuss. We don't have time to waste a-fussin'.

DONNA JUNE: You're right, Linda Jo. I could be the next one to go.

RHONDA RENAE: No, you won't! I told you, you'll be the last one—

DONNA JUNE: Rhonda Renae, hush! Let's don't fuss. We're friends, remember?

RHONDA RENAE: Yeah. We're friends. Have been for a long time . . . Let's don't quarrel. Don't want to leave here a-fussin' . . .

MUSIC in the background: "When the Roll is Called Up Yonder."

ANGEL A: Rhonda Renae.

RHONDA RENAE looks around with a smile. GIRLS' conversation fades and becomes pantomine, as before. RHONDA RENAE stands and goes to the front of the stage, as Vicki Lynn did.

RHONDA RENAE: *(brightens, looks around, smiles)* I hear music . . . heavenly music.

ANGEL A: Rhonda Renae . . . called to be a musician.

RHONDA RENAE: That's me. They're calling me. I'm going where the music is. They're calling me. They need me to play.

EXIT RHONDA RENAE. GIRLS' conversation fades in.

LISA MARIE: Why don't we have church now?

DONNA JUNE: Church? Now? Here?

LINDA JO: That's a good idea, Lisa Marie. We can sing. Rhonda Renae can play. Rhonda? Rhonda Renae? *(looks around)* Where is she?

DONNA JUNE: Don't tell me . . .

LISA MARIE: I'm afraid so. Rhonda Renae is gone, too. First Vicki Lynn left us. Now Rhonda Renae . . .

LINDA JO: I remember when all she knew how to play was "I Dropped My Dolly" and "Mary Had a Little Lamb."

LISA MARIE: I can't believe Rhonda Renae is gone.

DONNA JUNE: But she is. And a little music has left this earth.

LISA MARIE: *(surprised)* Why, Donna June, what a sweet thing to say.

DONNA JUNE: *(embarrassed)* Wellll, I said "a little music." I'm glad we were friends.

LINDA JO: *(aside)* She can't be softening in her old age!

DONNA JUNE: What did you say, Linda Jo?

LINDA JO: Never mind. Never mind.

DONNA JUNE: Lost my mind? Just because I said something nice you think I've lost my mind.

GIRLS pick up magazines and hide behind them.

ANGEL A: Lisa Marie . . .

LISA MARIE: *(jerks upright, wrinkles brow, looks upward)* Lisa Marie? Lisa Marie? Why, that's me. . . .

ANGEL A: Lisa Marie . . . called to be a wife and mother.

LISA MARIE: *(stands up, smiles and walks toward the exit)* That's me. I've got to go, but don't worry about me, girls. My Beloved is calling my name. I must go.

EXIT LISA MARIE

SILENCE for several seconds

LINDA JO: *(lowers magazine)* You ought to see this picture, Lisa Marie. I declare to my time, I don't know what this world is a'coming . . . . Lisa Marie? Donna June?

DONNA JUNE: *(peers over edge of magazine)* Heh?

LINDA JO: Did you see Lisa Marie leave?

DONNA JUNE: *(shocked)* No. No! She can't be gone—not Lisa Marie! Who's going to pray for me? I've always depended on Lisa Marie to pray. . . .

LINDA JO: I know. Donna June, don't you think it's time for you to pray?

DONNA JUNE: Me? Me pray? You mean, me be an intercessor like Lisa Marie?

LINDA JO: That's exactly what I mean.

DONNA JUNE: But that's not my role. I mean . . . I'm suppose to . . . I'm suppose to be a . . . uhhhhh . . . uhhhhh . . . *(wails)* Linda Jo, what am I suppose to be? I've never known. . . . All my life I've just drifted. I've been so sick . . . and unhappy. I never was happy and contented like Lisa Marie. . . .

LINDA JO: *(nods)* I know. Lisa Marie found her role and filled it. I've got a feeling she filled someone else's role, too.

DONNA JUNE: But I'm not talented like Rhonda Renae. I never could teach like Vicki Lynn. And I'm not like Lisa Marie. She was sweet and kind and—

LINDA JO: Lisa Marie's passing has left a gap. . . . Someone needs to make up the hedge, Donna June. Someone needs to take Lisa Marie's place.

DONNA JUNE: But I couldn't, could I? Some young person will have to do it. I mean I'm old and sick and . . . *(staggers to her feet)* And I've made excuses for myself too long. I could never take Lisa Marie's place, but I can fill my role. *(moves toward front center of stage)* Yep! It's never too late to start. It's time these old knees learned to bend.

DONNA JUNE kneels with her profile to audience.

LINDA JO: *(staggers to her feet)* Hmp! What'd you know about that! What'd you know about that!

EXIT LINDA JO

SONG: "Make Me What I Ought to Be" *(by congregation)*

EXIT DONNA JUNE, during song.

3

School Days
(An Allegory)

CAST
Students:
    Pastor's Wife "Denise" *(any age)*
    Mother "Linda" *(thirtyish)*
    Widow "Donna" *(sixtyish)*
    Single "Kendra" *(twentyish)*
    Grandmother "Tommye Kaye" *(fortyish)*
Teacher: Miss Comforter

PROPS
    5 backpacks
    school books, miscellaneous supplies
    chalkboard
    bell
    large trash can
    miscellaneous backpack fillers *(described later)*
    children's games, such as jacks, jump rope, etc.

STAGE SET-UP
    A teacher's desk is sitting at an angle to the audience. Five chairs or desks face it. Miscellaneous school items are scattered around the stage. Books, a bell, pencils, pads, etc. are on the teacher's desk. The chalkboard is placed in a prominent place where the audience can read it. The trash can is beside the desk.

SPECIAL INSTRUCTIONS: Each student carries a heavy load in her arms, plus a backpack on her back. SINGLE'S backpack and load is very light compared to the others.

Material in backpacks:
    ALL BACKPACKS: Bibles; black box *(worry)*; miscellaneous

items can be used for fillers underneath named items. Additional items needed are:

PASTOR'S WIFE: gaudy package *(pride)*, small heavy package *(inferiority)*, white package *(church)*;

MOTHER: tangled skein of yarn *(priorities)*, book on discipline *(guilt)*;

SINGLE: glittering package *(pride—this package and the black box of worry are added to her pack after Scene I)*;

GRANDMOTHER: sack of polyester filler;

WIDOW: tattered, ugly package *(grief)*.

Students may wear name tags around necks or on backpacks to identify them. Or the characters may be portrayed by ladies who are actually a widow, a mother, a pastor's wife, etc. Names of cast members may be used, especially if they are known by the audience. Of course, Miss Comforter must remain "Miss Comforter."

Scripts may be hidden in notebooks, carried by each along with school supplies. The teacher's script can be kept on her desk. For Scene III when she stands center stage and has a lot to say, she may carry her notebook with her. There are a few times when members of the cast will be positioned in such a place that they cannot use their script. These lines will need to be memorized. Of course, all should be so familiar with their parts that it will not be evident they are using a script.

Students should jump up and down quite a bit and make hand gestures so the audience can easily distinguish who is speaking. Also they should ad-lib in a natural way throughout the drama.

Scene I

My Load's Heavier Than Yours

ENTER TEACHER, writes on chalkboard, "WELCOME TO LIFE SCHOOL. Teacher: Miss Comforter." Takes seat at desk, shuffles through papers, looks at watch, and rings bell.

SOUND: SCHOOL BELL

ENTER STUDENTS, except SINGLE, from back coming up center aisle, staggering under loads and ad-libbing. There is considerable commotion as they drop items, stop to pick them up, etc. SINGLE ENTERS with her light load, singing and skipping around the others, and takes her seat in the classroom. As others near the front, they begin the script dialogue.

GRANDMOTHER: I don't see why she had to give us so much homework.

MOTHER: As if I didn't have enough *housework* already!

WIDOW: Well, there was just no way I could get it all done. I didn't have time.

MOTHER: You didn't have time? Of all people, you, Donna, should have had time. You don't have anyone but yourself to take care of.

WIDOW: *(sniffs)* Neither do I have a husband to help. . . .

TEACHER: *(stands and raps desk)* Students, please take your seats.

STUDENTS find chairs, grumbling and complaining. They have trouble adjusting their backpacks and the loads they are carrying, but they refuse to put anything down.

TEACHER: Good morning, girls.

CLASS: *(mumbles)* Morning.

PASTOR'S WIFE: *(yawns loudly)* That's the problem.

TEACHER: What's the problem, Denise?

PASTOR'S WIFE: It's morning! *(sings off-key)* "Oh, how I hate to get up in the morning. I'd much rather stay in bed." It seems like I'm always tired. *(yawns again)*

GRANDMOTHER: So am I. I never get enough rest.

MOTHER: What about me? I've got three kids and a husband to take care of, plus this staggering load of homework.

PASTOR'S WIFE: *(yawns)* I'm soooooo we-a- -r- -y. . . . *(drifts off to sleep, snores occasionally).*

WIDOW: You all are not the only ones who are exhausted. I've been under this load of grief for so long that I am drained.

GRANDMOTHER: How long has it been since you lost your husband, Donna?

WIDOW: Sixteen years, fourteen months, forty-eight days, six hours, fifteen minutes, and *(looks at watch)* fifty-two seconds.

GRANDMOTHER: My, my, that is a long time to carry such a load.

MOTHER: Teacher, why do you give us so much homework? You know we're loaded down already.

GRANDMOTHER: On top of being soooo weary! I thought when I got my kids raised I'd get a break, but now instead of three kids to take care of, I've got six. They multiply, you know! I had to babysit five of my grandchildren last night. You ought to try finding a quiet time in a mob like that!

WIDOW: Did you get your homework done, Kendra?

SINGLE: Sure, it wasn't that har . . . *(begins to stammer as others glare at her)* I . . . I . . . I mean . . . well . . . most . . . most . . . of it . . . .

MOTHER: *(shrugs)* Well, you should get yours done. After all, you don't have anything else to do.

SINGLE: I certainly do, too. I have to support myself.

MOTHER: *(scornfully)* Yourself? Sure, but that's all.

SINGLE: All? I don't have anyone to help me. I have to make all the decisions.

MOTHER: What's so bad about that? When you have a husband, the only decision you get to make is when to change the baby.

WIDOW: Where is your homework anyway, Kendra? Your backpack looks awfully light to me!

SINGLE: Well . . . I . . . I . . .

PASTOR'S WIFE: *(yawns and stretches)* That helped a little bit. What are we talking about?

TEACHER: Class, I want to—

WIDOW: We're talking about Kendra's backpack. Look at her!

PASTOR'S WIFE: Hummmm . . . You must not be very dedicated or you would have a heavier load than that.

SINGLE: But I am. And my load is heavier than it looks. I have to make all the money, pay all the bills—

PASTOR'S WIFE: At our house there's never enough money to pay the bills. Did you know that preachers are the lowest paid professionals on the chart? That's one reason my load is so heavy. We're always having a financial crisis.

WIDOW: You don't know how blessed you are. You ought to have my load and try to live on a fixed income.

PASTOR'S WIFE: At least your income is fixed. Ours is broken!

GRANDMOTHER: What's the matter with you, Kendra, that you aren't all burdened down like we are?

SINGLE: Well, I . . . uhhhh . . . I am. It's just that—

WIDOW: It's just that she's never been through any tough tests like the rest of us.

MOTHER: She doesn't have any housework so of course she can get her homework done. *(waves hand furiously)* Teacher? Teacher?

TEACHER: Yes, Linda?

MOTHER: Didn't Professor Paul write in the Textbook that singles ought to do double homework?

TEACHER: I think you have misinterpreted Paul's—

GRANDMOTHER: He certainly did. Because singles don't have a husband to take care of, they ought to be twice as loaded as we who are married.

163

PASTOR'S WIFE: *(clicks tongue, shakes finger at Single)* They're right, you know. You really ought to get under the load.

SINGLE: But I do . . . I mean, I am. I never miss a class. I always hand in my homework on time. I study. I work.

GRANDMOTHER: *(jumps to feet)* Brag! Brag! Brag! Young lady, you had better beware or pride will be your downfall. *Let him that thinketh he standeth take heed lest (slips and falls, gets up and finishes) lest he fall.* I read that in the Textbook.

SINGLE: I'm sorry. I didn't realize I—

GRANDMOTHER: If I was you, Kendra, I'd find something else to add to my pack. It doesn't look good to have the lightest load. Every good student is overloaded these days. You know it's a status symbol to be stressed out.

WIDOW: *(sighs deeply)* I'm sure I have the heaviest load of anyone I know.

MOTHER: You? Why your load doesn't begin to compare to mine. I've got two teenagers and a toddler!

PASTOR'S WIFE: If you think your load is heavy, you ought to have to carry mine. I mean, I've got all my problems, plus the problems of everyone in the church. No one knows what a tremendous load I carry!

GIRLS begin to argue, voices raising, "Mine's the heaviest," "No mine," "Just try lifting mine," etc. for a few seconds.

TEACHER: Girls . . . girls! *(shouts)* GIRLS!

SILENCE

TEACHER: Why won't you listen when I speak to you in a quiet voice? Why must I shout?

SOUND: BELL

TEACHER: We have wasted this entire class. It's time for recess.

STUDENTS begin getting up under loads, dropping things, picking them up, trying to adjust packs so they can leave.

TEACHER: Why don't you leave your burdens here during recess?

STUDENTS: *(shocked)* WHAT? LEAVE OUR PRECIOUS BURDENS? OH, NO! WE COULD NEVER DO THAT!

As TEACHER talks, STUDENTS pick up and adjust loads, then stagger out one by one, ignoring her.

TEACHER: But, girls, you need a break. You need to rest. I planned recess for your enjoyment. Girls? GIRLS? GIRLS??? *(shrugs)* How can you talk to someone who won't listen?

EXIT ALL

Scene II

Comfort Ye, My People

ENTER TEACHER, sits down at desk.

SOUND: BELL

ENTER STUDENTS, from back, staggering under loads, as before. SINGLE walks stooped over; her pack is bulging with items added between scenes, including worry and pride.

TEACHER: Take your seats quickly and quietly, please.

STUDENTS take seats, shuffling loads, but clinging to them stubbornly.

TEACHER: Did you enjoy recess?

GRANDMOTHER: Enjoy it? How could we enjoy it, carrying these heavy loads?

PASTOR'S WIFE: I'm wearier now than I was before recess. Even breaks wear me out. *(yawns)*

WIDOW: You're weary, Denise? What about me? My heart just gets heavier every day.

TEACHER: Donna, if you would let me, I would—

MOTHER: You should have spent the night walking the floor like I did. I was so burdened I couldn't sleep.

SINGLE: What's the problem, Linda?

MOTHER: I was worried sick about Jennifer, my three-year-old.

SINGLE: What's the matter with her? Is she sick?

MOTHER: Oh, no, she's in perfect health. *(wrings hands)* I'm just afraid she's going to get involved with the wrong crowd and get pregnant or catch AIDS or have something terrible happen to her.

GRANDMOTHER: I understand your fears perfectly, Linda. You can't begin to worry about them too soon. Why I started worrying about mine before they were born, and I'll tell you I didn't start a minute too soon. They've given me cause for every worry I ever had. *(sighs heavily)* And now I've got to start all over with six grandchildren!

PASTOR'S WIFE: Well, like I said, I've got all my worries and everyone else's too. No one knows how heavy a load I carry.

TEACHER: I told you to leave your packs with me.

GRANDMOTHER: But, Miss Comforter, you know we can't put them down.

WIDOW: What would people think if they saw us out there, laughing and enjoying ourselves without our burdens? They'd think we . . . we . . . we . . .

PASTOR'S WIFE: They'd think we were backslidden! I mean, they'd think we didn't care.

WIDOW: That's right! They'd think we weren't even worried. And goodness knows, there's enough to worry about these days.

SINGLE: Does anyone notice anything different about me?

PASTOR'S WIFE: Ahhhh, no, I can't say . . . Well, maybe there is a difference. Yes, there is! You're more stooped and solemn looking.

Why, girls, look at Kendra's backpack! She's got a real, honest-to-goodness load!

SINGLE: Girls, I'm trying. I really am. I've got such a happy-go-lucky nature that it's really hard for me to worry, but I'm working on it.

GIRLS, all except SINGLE, stagger to their feet and chant verse in singsong voice, clapping time.

GIRLS: Kendra Sue, hooray for you!
You have learned to worry, too!
Kendra Sue, we're proud of you!

GIRLS pat SINGLE on the back and shake her hand, then awkward-ly sit down.

PASTOR'S WIFE: Now that you've got more than you can carry, you look like a genuine student!

GRANDMOTHER: Isn't it great that we are all so heavy laden?

WIDOW: Heavy laden? Now where did I read that? *(scratches head)*

MOTHER: In a book on prenatal care?

WIDOW: No, it's been years since I read a book on prenatal care. . . . It seems like just the other day I read that . . . heavy laden. Now where was it?

TEACHER: How about your Textbook, Donna?

WIDOW: Textbook? Oh, yeah. . . . It said something about being heavy laden and weary and I thought—boy, that sure fits me. Now what else did it say?

TEACHER: It's time for a lesson. Turn in your Textbook to Matthew 11:28.

GIRLS dig in backpacks until they find their Bibles. They pull them out and find verse of Scripture.

TEACHER: Kendra, do you have it?

SINGLE: Yes, here it is. *Come unto me, all ye that labour and are heavy laden . . .*

WIDOW: That's it. That's it. Sure fits us, doesn't it, girls?

PASTOR'S WIFE: I'll say so. "Ye that labour and are heavy laden" is a perfect fit.

TEACHER: Read the rest of the verse.

GRANDMOTHER: Like I said, it's wonderful we're all so heavy laden. We can be a great comfort to one another.

TEACHER: Denise, read the rest of the verse.

MOTHER: Look at the clock. We'd better start home.

TEACHER: Girls! Finish the verse!

MOTHER: As loaded as we are, it will take awhile to get there.

TEACHER: GIRLS!

GIRLS: *(look at teacher)* Yes, Miss Comforter?

TEACHER: Why do you think I'm here?

GIRLS shrug shoulders and look at one another in bewilderment.

WIDOW: Why are you here?

TEACHER: To teach you if you would listen—to guide you and to comfort you.

WIDOW: Oh, don't worry about that, Miss Comforter. We have each other. We'll make it.

GRANDMOTHER: Now, girls, we'd better get started. It's a long, hard road home.

GIRLS gather up loads, helping one another, ad-libbing as they do so. As they stagger out . . .

SINGLE: *(looks up at sky)* You know there's not a cloud in sight, but I can't help but worry. What if a tornado strikes before we get home?

GIRLS: *(chant as they EXIT)*
　　　　Kendra Sue, hooray for you!
　　　　You have learned to worry too.
　　　　Kendra Sue, we're proud of you!

TEACHER: *(stands)* Comfort ye, comfort ye, my people . . . but they would not hear.

EXIT TEACHER

Scene III

A Look in the Backpacks

ENTER TEACHER, sits at desk.

SOUND: BELL

ENTER STUDENTS, staggering, dropping items, helping one another pick up things, then dropping more, ad-libbing as they come up the center aisle. When they get to the stage . . .

WIDOW: I slept ten hours last night, and I'm still worn out. I tell you my load gets heavier every day. It's almost unbearable.

GRANDMOTHER: I know. If the teacher would just stop loading us down . . . I feel so weak and exhausted.

MOTHER: She ought to know I don't have time for homework. Just look at this stack of unfinished assignments.

PASTOR'S WIFE: I guess if we'd ever finish an assignment, our workload would get lighter. But who can do homework when you are drained?

SINGLE: Come to think of it, Miss Comforter didn't give us an assignment yesterday.

WIDOW: Or the day before . . . In fact, I can't remember the last time she did give us an assignment.

GRANDMOTHER: Hummmm . . . I guess the truth is she has only given us one assignment, but we were supposed to do it every day. Can anyone remember what it was?

PASTOR'S WIFE: It was so long ago. . . . Oh, what was it? *(snaps fingers)* Now, I remember. It was—*Fear God, and keep his commandments: for this is the whole duty of man* (Ecclesiastes 12:13).

WIDOW: That's it! "Fear God, and keep his commandments." Then why is my load heavier than it was yesterday?

PASTOR'S WIFE: Maybe because you haven't been doing your homework.

TEACHER: *(stands)* Girls, please take your seats.

GIRLS stagger to seats, as before.

TEACHER: Good morning, girls.

GIRLS: *(mumble)* Morning.

TEACHER: You girls always look like you are exhausted.

PASTOR'S WIFE: *(yawns)* That's because we are.

TEACHER: Why do you come to class so burdened down?

GIRLS: Why?

PASTOR'S WIFE: Miss Comforter, are you asking us why? You are the one who loads us down.

TEACHER: I load you down? Oh, no. Not with the burdens you bear, I don't. I've been trying to tell you that if you would let me, I would give you rest.

GIRLS: *(yell)* Rest?

SINGLE: You mean, the rest of our homework? Oh, no! All you ever give us is homework.

TEACHER: I mean rest from your weariness. I never lay on you a greater burden than the necessary things. All I ever ask of you is reasonable service. "Fear God . . ."

GIRLS: *(moan)* "And keep his commandments." We know.

WIDOW: I wouldn't call this load I am carrying "reasonable."

TEACHER: Neither would I, Donna. That is why today we are going to clean out your backpacks.

GIRLS: *(shocked, grab packs as if protecting them)* CLEAN OUT OUR BACKPACKS?

WIDOW: *(wails)* But you can't do that! I haven't touched mine since my beloved Calvin died sixteen years, fourteen months, forty-eight, I mean forty-nine days, eight hours *(peers at watch)*, ninety-three minutes, and fifty-two seconds ago.

TEACHER: Then it's time to lighten your load.

WIDOW: But . . . but . . . I . . . I . . . he'd think I didn't love him. I mean, people would think I didn't love him.

SINGLE: And I just filled my pack yesterday. My load was so light everyone said I must be half-hearted and lukewarm. "Every diligent student carries a heavy, heavy load," they said.

TEACHER: Let's look at what you added to your pack, Kendra.

SINGLE and TEACHER meet center front stage. SINGLE pulls out large black box.

TEACHER: Just what I thought. You don't need that.

GIRLS: Don't need it? We don't need worry?

TEACHER: You don't need to carry worry. Worry is an unproductive weight that should be cast aside.

SINGLE: But I thought every good, consecrated, conscientious, diligent student worried. I mean, what if I fail? What if there's an earthquake and I can't get to school? What if the sky falls in? What if I forget my lines?

TEACHER: I want everyone of you to take worry out of your packs and throw it away.

MOTHER: But, Miss Comforter, are you sure? You know my children are pretty young. I've got a lot of good worrying days ahead of me.

WIDOW: And what about me? I've got to paddle my own canoe. What if I get caught in a whirlpool?

TEACHER: The Master Teacher said, *Take no thought saying, What shall we eat? or, What shall we drink? or, Wherewithal shall we be clothed? . . . for your heavenly Father knoweth that ye have need of all these things* (Matthew 6:31-32). Worry is unbelief. And you can never make a passing grade carrying a load of unbelief and worry. So throw it away now!

Each student takes a black box out of her pack. Reluctantly they throw the boxes in the trash can beside the teacher's desk.

WIDOW: I've carried it so long, I'm not sure I can. . . .

SINGLE: I feel better already. Almost like my old joyful self. But there's still something bulky in here.

TEACHER: Let's see it.

SINGLE: *(pulls out glittering package)* It's pride. I only put it in because I didn't want anyone thinking I wasn't as spiritual . . . I mean, scholarly, as everyone else. *(throws package in trash, straightens shoulders and smiles)* I feel good! Strong and joyful.

SINGLE sits down.

TEACHER: Let's look in your pack, Tommye Kaye.

GRANDMOTHER joins TEACHER in center stage. Teacher opens Grandmother's pack. She holds up a bag of polyester filler for all to see. GIRLS gasp in amazement.

172

WIDOW: *(stands up and shakes finger at Grandmother)* I thought you were carrying a load. You sure put on a good show. Staggering around and complaining, whining and pretending like your load was as heavy as ours . . . and all the time . . . all the time you were carrying a load of fluff! *(sits down in disgust)*

GRANDMOTHER: *(on verge of tears)* But it felt heavy. My back hurts and my shoulders ache. Even my knees are trembly.

TEACHER: *(puts arm around Grandmother)* That's because you are weak, my dear. You haven't been eating a balanced diet or getting the right kind of exercise.

GRANDMOTHER: *(sniffing and sobbing)* But I'm so busy with the grandchildren and all my projects, I don't have time to worry about diet and exercise.

TEACHER: You've got to start taking time. You need some good strong meat. And deep knee bends every day would do you a world of good. *(Grandmother does a few knee-bends and groans loudly.)* Before you know it, you will be strong enough to carry a real load.

GRANDMOTHER: *(smiles and hugs Teacher)* Yes, ma'am. I'll start today. *(throws polyester filler in trash and takes seat.)*

TEACHER: Who is next?

PASTOR'S WIFE: *(staggers to feet and take her place by Teacher)* I doubt if there is anything in my pack that can be disposed of. You know, Miss Comforter, that if I lay anything down, the whole church will fall to pieces!

TEACHER: *(smiles gently)* We'll see.

TEACHER and PASTOR'S WIFE open pack. As they dig . . .

PASTOR'S WIFE: Remember I've already thrown worry away, and I just don't think I can. . . .

TEACHER holds up gaudy package.

TEACHER: I see Kendra is not the only one carrying pride.

PASTOR'S WIFE: But . . . but . . . but . . . I . . . I'm the PASTOR'S WIFE!

TEACHER: I know, and the Textbook says, *Whosoever will be chief among you, let him be your servant* (Matthew 20:27). And servants don't need pride. So let's throw it away. *(tosses package in trash)*

PASTOR'S WIFE: *(sighs)* Maybe you're right. I sure do get tired of trying to be Mrs. Perfect all the time.

TEACHER: *(hugs Pastor's Wife)* I know I'm right. Anything else in there you want to get rid of?

PASTOR'S WIFE: *(searches bag, holds up tiny package)* Look what I found. It was hidden by pride. *(hands package to Teacher)* It's little, but it's awfully heavy.

TEACHER: Inferiority

PASTOR'S WIFE: Other pastor's wives are so . . . so . . . first-class. I mean . . . you know . . . they can do everything, and I can't even bake a decent pie. Mine are always the last to sell at the bake sales. I've felt inferior for years, but I've managed to keep it pretty well hidden by pride. But now that pride's gone, I guess it's time to get rid of inferiority too.

TEACHER: *(throws package in trash and hugs Pastor's Wife)* Feel better?

PASTOR'S WIFE: Sure do. I'm not nearly as tired as I was. Trying to be someone you're not is really very, very tiring . . . *(stops and thinks a second, then adds very pointedly)* on yourself and everyone else, too. *(returns to seat, starts to sit down, then stands back up)* Miss Comforter, what about the church? What's going to happen to the church now that I . . . ? *(pulls white package out of backpack)*

TEACHER: The Master Teacher can take care of it. It's His.

PASTOR'S WIFE: Ooooohhhh, I never thought of that. *(gives package to Teacher, smiles and sits down)*

TEACHER: *(lays white package on desk, turns to class)* Linda, it's your turn.

MOTHER: *(joins Teacher in center stage, shaking head)* I don't see how I can get rid of my children!

TEACHER: *(laughs)* Don't worry. We won't throw them away. They're blessings, not burdens.

BOTH look in Mother's pack. TEACHER pulls out a mass of tangled yarn.

TEACHER: What is this?

MOTHER: Looks like my tangled nerves.

TEACHER: I'd say it's your mixed-up priorities. That's what tangles up your nerves. These are in such a mess, I suggest you throw them away and start all over.

MOTHER: But how did they get like that? I started right.

TEACHER: Oh, little by little . . . a knot here and a twist there. Remember, Linda, houses keep but children don't. You don't have to have a spotless house. Your children don't have to wear name-brand clothes. They don't have to have a computer and a swimming pool. But they do need your time, your ear, and your example.

MOTHER: *(puts hands to face)* Oh, I know. I know, but I keep forgetting. The pressure is to be the best, wear the best, have the best. . . .

TEACHER: *(pats her shoulder)* But the best according to the Master Teacher is love, not things. What else are you carrying that you don't need?

MOTHER: *(pulls out book on discipline)* Guilt. I feel so guilty all the time. If I spank my children, I feel like a child abuser. If I don't discipline them, I feel like a weakling. Whatever I do, I wonder if it was right. The more books I read, the heavier my load gets. I'm getting a complex about giving my children a complex.

TEACHER: *(nods)* Raising children is a complex business. Go to the Textbook for your instructions. Now let's throw guilt away. *(throws book in trash)* Remember just ask the Master Teacher for help and do your best. That's all anyone can do.

MOTHER: *(throws arms around Teacher)* Oh, you're such a comfort to me! *(returns to seat)*

WIDOW stands up reluctantly and meets TEACHER in center stage.

WIDOW: My turn. But, Miss Comforter, I don't know what dear Calvin would say about this.

TEACHER: He would say that he wants you to be happy. Now let's throw that grief away, Donna.

WIDOW: *(starts to pull out ugly black package, hesitates)* But I can't give him up. . . .

TEACHER: You aren't giving him up. You still have your memories and they are light. They won't burden you down. But after sixteen years, it's time to get rid of grief. *(holds out hand)* Let it go, Donna. The Master Teacher bore your grief and carried your sorrow a long time ago. There's no need for you to spend the rest of your life carrying it.

WIDOW: *(slowly hands over package, then smiles)* There! I did it! I did it! Say, look outside. *(points)*

TEACHER: What?

WIDOW: The sun is shining!

TEACHER: *(laughs)* It has been, Donna, for sixteen years, fourteen months, and forty-nine days. *(hugs her)*

BOTH return to seats. TEACHER looks at watch.

TEACHER: Would you believe it is almost time for recess? Now, girls, why don't you leave the rest of your burdens with me? I am quite capable of taking care of them.

SINGLE: *(jumps up, takes off backpack)* I'll do it, Miss Comforter. I feel so much better already. I'd like to get rid of all my burdens. *(lays pack on Teacher's desk)*

PASTOR'S WIFE: *(takes off backpack)* I feel so rested. I feel like running and shouting and playing. *(lays pack on desk)*

WIDOW, GRANDMOTHER and MOTHER take off packs and put them on the desk. GIRLS join hands and EXIT singing, "All of my burdens went rolling away. . . ."

Scene IV

My Burden is Light

ENTER STUDENTS. Some are jumping rope, others play jacks or hopscotch (any outdoor action game played by schoolgirls will do). They are ad-libbing, playing, laughing as TEACHER ENTERS. She smiles, takes seat at desk, glances at watch.

SOUND: BELL

STUDENTS continue laughing and playing, ignoring bell.

SOUND: BELL

STUDENTS ignore bell. TEACHER frowns, picks up bell, walks to center stage and rings bell loudly several times. STUDENTS continue playing.

TEACHER: *(calls loudly)* Girls! Time for class. *(no response, games continue)* GIRLS! TIME FOR CLASS!

GRANDMOTHER: I think Miss Comforter is calling us.

TEACHER: GIRLS! TIME FOR CLASS!

WIDOW: Oh, no. I haven't had this much fun in years. Who wants to study?

SINGLE: Why don't we skip school this afternoon?

GRANDMOTHER: *(chuckles)* It's been a long time since I've done that.

SINGLE: Too late. She's watching us.

TEACHER: GIRLS! COME IN THIS INSTANT!

177

GIRLS stop playing, gather up toys and take seats, grumbling and complaining. TEACHER stands behind desk.

PASTOR'S WIFE: Just when we get out from under our burdens and start having a good time, you call us in to study.

GRANDMOTHER: *(huffing and puffing)* Just that . . . little bit of ex-er-cise . . . has made me feel bet-ter. I don't need . . . to sit here and study. I need to play . . . and get ex-er-cise.

TEACHER: There is a time to play and a time to study. *(sits down at desk and flips through Textbook, without looking up, says)* Turn in your Textbooks to yesterday's lesson, Matthew 11:28-30.

PASTOR'S WIFE and SINGLE whisper and giggle. MOTHER throws spit wads at GRANDMOTHER. WIDOW sits daydreaming.

TEACHER: *(looks up)* GIRLS! I am asking you to pay attention.

GIRLS continue giggling, playing, whispering, etc.

TEACHER: *(gets up from desk, picks up a backpack from the pile beside her desk)* Come forward and get your backpacks! *(repeats in louder, sterner voice)* Come forward and get your backpacks!

GIRLS look at her in shock.

GRANDMOTHER: What did you say, Miss Comforter?

TEACHER: I said, come forward and get your backpacks, now.

SINGLE: But . . . but . . . but you told us to take them off!

TEACHER: For recess. Now it's time to get back in the harness.

GIRLS: Ohhhhhhh, no!

MOTHER: It feels sooooo good to be without that load, I'll never put it back on.

WIDOW: Neither will I. I haven't felt this lighthearted in sixteen years. I'm not about to put that thing back on!

GIRLS: *(shake heads and voice agreement)*

TEACHER: *(sighs and sits down on edge of desk, holding a backpack)* Before recess we cleaned out your backpacks and got rid of all your self-made burdens.

PASTOR'S WIFE: Self-made burdens?

TEACHER: Yes, self-made burdens. Weights you were carrying that you didn't have to carry, worry, pride, grief . . .

MOTHER: Guilt . . .

TEACHER: *(nods)* Right. They only burdened you down. They were unproductive weights. But there are still some things in your backpacks.

SINGLE: Spare me.

TEACHER: I would if I could, and to a large extent I can. When you brought your backpacks to me, you learned a valuable lesson.

PASTOR'S WIFE: Yeah. *(sings)* "Take your burden to the teacher and leave it there."

SINGLE: That's what I'm going to do . . . leave it there. No more backpacks for me.

MOTHER: Me, either.

TEACHER: Do you mean, Linda, that you wish to be free of your family?

MOTHER: Yes . . . *(horrified)* Oh, I mean, no! Never!

TEACHER: Then you must take up your backpack again. You have thrown out worry and guilt, but you still must bear responsibility. It is a load life places on us all. You, Kendra, still have to provide for yourself and make your own decisions.

MOTHER: What's so bad about that? Like I said, when you are married, the only—

TEACHER: Linda, I was talking.

MOTHER: *(mumbles)* Sorry.

TEACHER: I repeat, life places burdens on us. Our loved ones die. Our children stray away from what we have taught them. Homes fall apart. These are the burdens of life, and no one completely escapes them. I can't spare you these burdens, but I can help you carry them.

GRANDMOTHER: I'd be glad to let you carry the whole load. I'm stronger, but I don't think I'm strong enough to pick up my load yet.

TEACHER: You must bear your own burden, but I will walk right along beside you and strengthen you . . . if you will let me. *(goes back behind desk and picks up Textbook)* Now turn in your Textbooks to yesterday's reading lesson, Matthew 11:28-30.

ALL find verses in Bibles.

TEACHER: Read verse 28, please, Denise.

PASTOR'S WIFE: *Come unto me, all ye that labour and are heavy laden.* . . .

TEACHER: That's as far as we got yesterday. But listen to the rest of this verse.

PASTOR'S WIFE: *And I will give you rest.* Say, that's what you did. You gave us rest. I haven't felt this relaxed in years.

TEACHER: That's because it has been years since you cast your burdens on me. Now, Donna, read verse 29, please.

WIDOW: *Take my yoke upon you, and learn of me; for I am meek and lowly in heart: and ye shall find rest unto your souls.*

TEACHER: See why pride is such a burden? The Master Teacher was meek and lowly in heart. Pride is a heavy weight that robs us of rest.

WIDOW: But I don't like the first part of that verse, *Take my yoke upon you.* I don't want to take anything else upon me. I like this light, free feeling.

TEACHER. We need to read the next verse. Let's read it together.

ALL: *For my yoke is easy, and my burden is light.*

MOTHER: A light burden? I'd like to see it.

TEACHER: *(holds backpack out toward class)* Here it is. Come and get it.

MOTHER: But that's just one of our old backpacks.

TEACHER: I know. We have thrown out all the self-made burdens. During recess while you renewed your strength, I lightened life's burdens for you, and now I want you to take upon you the burden of the Lord.

GIRLS: The burden of the Lord?

PASTOR'S WIFE: I thought that was what I was carrying all the time . . . but I guess it wasn't. I didn't realize I had manufactured my own burdens.

GRANDMOTHER: What is the burden of the Lord?

TEACHER: A desire to see the lost saved, a hunger for revival, a love for holiness, a zeal to study, a longing to pray. . . .

PASTOR'S WIFE: Say, that sounds like our homework: *Fear God, and keep his commandments.*

TEACHER: And so it is. Who wants to be first to take on you the burden of the Lord? *(no response)* Remember the last verse? *For my yoke is easy, and my burden is light.*

PASTOR'S WIFE: Well, I guess I should be first. After all, I'm the pastor's wife. I'm supposed to be the example. *(stands, goes forward and puts on old backpack—wiggles experimentally, straightens shoulders, and smiles broadly)* I can't believe it, girls! I can hardly feel it. It is light. It is.

OTHERS quickly come forward and put on backpacks. Stand straight, smiling, ad-libbing, line up in front.

WIDOW: I can't believe it is the same old backpack.

TEACHER: Well, it is, Donna. But it's not the same old load.

PASTOR'S WIFE: Girls, can you believe it took us this long to learn this one simple lesson?

TEACHER: *(smiling)* Oh, you didn't do so bad. It takes some people a lifetime to learn it. And some never do.

SOUND: BELL

TEACHER: Lesson learned. Class dismissed.

GIRLS curtsy and EXIT.

SONG: "Come unto Me" *(by congregation)*

4

The Race

CAST
>   Time
>   Traveler, dressed as jogger
>   Worry, dressed in black
>   Past, dressed in Scene I as a ghost, in other scenes as Granny

PROPS
>   clock that ticks loudly
>   child's scooter
>   cross
>   2 chairs
>   end table
>   roll of computer paper, containing script of Scene I
>   map, containing script of Scene II
>   paper sack

Scene   I: The CROSSroads (Past)
Scene II: The Road Ahead (Future)
Scene III: EnJOYing the Trip (Present)

SONGS
>   "Give Them All to Jesus"
>   "I Don't Know about Tomorrow"
>   "We Have This Moment, Today"
>   "In the Presence of the Lord"

INSTRUCTIONS: Directions are given from stage facing the audience.

Ticking of the clock is heard in background constantly. To do this place a clock beside a hidden microphone.

Scene I: The CROSSroads

The Past

STAGE SETTING: Podium is placed on right front. The cross is in the back center.

ENTER TIME, dressed in white or light blue robe, hair in disarray, glasses slipping down on nose. Rushes to the podium and collapses on it.

TIME: I hope I don't feel as old as I look . . . I mean, look as old as I feel. I'm just about worn to a frazzle. Will I ever get to rest? Maybe . . . in eternity . . . but I wouldn't count on it. Someone is sure to smuggle a clock into Heaven.

I guess if anyone has a right to look worn out and wrinkled and weary, it's me. After all, I've been around a long time. In fact, I was born in the beginning . . . that's right, "the beginning."

My birth announcement is Genesis 1:1. No doubt you've read it many times, but never connected it with me. But right there I am: "In the beginning."

The beginning . . . my beginning . . . the beginning of TIME.

And not long after I—Time—began, God created man, and that was the beginning of my problems.

Now humans are natural dividers. They dissect and divide and cut and—cut up. So they divided me into three parts—past, present, and future.

But that was still pretty vague for people's analytical minds—so they cut me up some more . . . centuries, years, months, weeks, days, hours, minutes, seconds—now, they're even talking about milliseconds.

Then they invented clocks and calendars so they could measure me . . . and measure me . . . and measure me. (No lady my age likes to be measured!)

People call my past, "history," my future "prophecy," and my present . . . well, they're not too interested in that. It's my past and my future, yesterday and tomorrow, that people are concerned about. They're running from the past and worrying about the future. The present is . . . well, the present is just to be "gotten through."

ENTER TRAVELER, from back, wearing jogging clothes (jean skirt, sweat shirt, tennis shoes, headband, large stopwatch), has rolled-up strip of computer paper (script on it) tucked under her belt.

TRAVELER: *(dragging as if she had been running a long time, huff-*

ing and puffing; holds wrist in front of face, stares at watch, counting seconds. Speaks in gasps.) Forty-two, forty-three, forty-four, forty-five, forty-WHEW! I've got to catch my breath. *(takes several deep breaths, keeps jogging)* Fifty-six, fifty-seven, fifty-eight, fifty-nine, three minutes! I did it! Three minutes without stopping!

TRAVELER starts onto stage—sees TIME.

TRAVELER: *(still gasping)* La-dee-dah. Well, good morning. And who are you?

TIME: I am Time.

TRAVELER: Pleased to meet you, I'm sure. Now if you'll just move over out of the way, I'm in a hur—Time? Time! You're Time? I thought Time was a father.

TIME: Not any more. These are the days of equal rights. I am Mother Time.

TRAVELER: You mean hours, minutes, seconds. That kinda time?

TIME: *(nods)* That kind of time.

TRAVELER: Then you're the one I've been racing.

TIME: I expect so. Most people are.

TRAVELER: Well! Well! I never expected to meet you. In fact I never thought I'd catch up with you. What's the matter? Have you slowed down?

TIME: No. I'm the same as always. May I ask . . . what's the rush?

TRAVELER: Well, you ought to know. You're the one who's pushing me. There's not much time and—

TIME: Not much time? There's all the time in the world.

TRAVELER: Maybe for you, but not for me. I've got to hurry.

TIME: Where are you going?

TRAVELER: Going? Where am I going? Well, I'm going to . . . uhhhh . . . I'm going to uhhhhh . . . I'm going to eternity.

TIME: Going to eternity? I am, too. We all are. But you seem to be in a hurry to get there.

TRAVELER: In a hurry to get there? To eternity? Well . . . well, not really, but . . . but . . . Say, I'm sorry to cut this short, but I've got a lot of ground to cover, and tomorrow's another day. *(jogs to center stage)*

TIME: *(to audience)* Tomorrow's another day? Well, I hope so.

TRAVELER: *(still gasping, jogging in place)* Now, let's see, where's my route itinerary? *(pulls roll out from belt and unfolds list)* Hummmmmmm . . . *(peers at bottom of list)* Three hundred thirty-eight things to do . . . I mean, miles to go . . . about a normal day. But wait, I've only got three hundred thirty-seven and seven-eighths things to . . . miles to go. I've already covered an eighth of a mile this morning—one-eighth of a mile in three minutes. . . . Wonder if that sets some kind of a record? Let's see, eight times three equals sixteen. No. That's not right. Eight times three equals twenty-two? No. Twenty-four? That's it, twenty-four. That's one mile in twenty-four minutes. Hummmmm, that's not quite three miles an hour . . . and I've got three hundred thirty-seven and seven-eighths miles to go today! Man, I've got to get some wheels! *(jogs faster as she talks)* Faster! Faster! Faster! *(dashes out)*

SOUND: *TICKING OF CLOCK*

ENTER TRAVELER, riding a scooter, followed by the GHOST OF THE PAST, who stands in the background.

TRAVELER: There! That's better. Now I can get somewhere. Maybe I can cover all three hundred thirty-seven and seven-eighths on this. *(rides scooter around in circles on stage)* Whew! Look at me! I'm makin' tracks!

TIME: Yeah, but you aren't going anywhere.

TRAVELER: Not going anywhere? I certainly am . . . I'm moving. I can feel the wind blowing through my hair . . . I am going . . . I am going . . . to have a wreck.

TIME: You're going in circles! You'll never make it under your own power. Why don't you let—

TRAVELER: See what I said? You're always pushing me.

As TRAVELER passes PAST. PAST reaches out and grabs TRAVELER and stops her. TRAVELER almost falls.

TRAVELER: *(pulls away from Past)* What? Hey, what's the idea? Who are you?

PAST: *(leans forward, hand cupped around ear)* How do you do? I'm fine, thank you.

TRAVELER: *(louder)* I said who are you.

PAST: Whooooo am I? Why, I am the Past . . . your past.

TRAVELER: The Past? *(weakly)* My past? But you can't be. I ran away from you a long time ago.

PAST: Speak up, youngun. Speak up! My hearin's not what it used to be.

TRAVELER: I said you can't be my past. I ran away from you a long time ago.

PAST: Yoooooou ran away from me? That's what you thought. I've always been in the background . . . watching . . . waiting. *(points at cross)* I knew sooner or later we'd meet at the crossroads. Yoooooooou need to do a little backtracking.

TRAVELER: *(wipes sweat from brow)* But you can't bother me now. I don't have time to deal with you. I've got to go forward.

PAST: You've got to run the lawn mower?

TRAVELER: *(louder)* I said you can't bother me now. I don't have time to deal with you. I've got to go forward.

PAST: *(grabs Traveler)* You'll never make any progress going forward until you have dealt with me. Now why are you running from me?

TRAVELER: Why? You don't know? Yes, you know! *(bitterly)* Remember . . . remember what . . . what they did to me? *(points at heart)* Just look . . . see the scars? They did that to me when I was just a kid . . . I was just a little girl! *(sobs—horrified)* And remember . . . remember what I did? I was just young and stupid. I didn't know any better. *(sorrowfully)* Yes, I did! I knew better, but I did it anyway . . . and now I can't forget. And I can't forgive. I can't forgive them . . . and I can't forgive myself. And you ask me why! *(sobs)* Why am I running away from you? Because of the pain . . . I can't handle the pain! I can't handle it! I can't face it! I can't! I can't!

TRAVELER breaks loose from the PAST, drops scooter, and runs from the stage.

PAST: *(turns to Time)* It's always this way. They'll never face me. I only want to make peace with her. I have so many wonderful memories to show her—if only she would stop and listen.

TIME: Give her time. Give her time.

PAST: Liver's a dime? But whoooo likes liver?

TIME: I said give her time. Give her time.

PAST: But that's what bothers me. She's wasting precious time—running from me. As long as I haunt her, she misses the present and fears the future.

TIME: I know. I know . . . But listen . . .

SONG: "Give Them All to Jesus"

As music begins, TRAVELER ENTERS, picks up scooter and slowly starts going around and around.

At the end of the first verse, TRAVELER lays down scooter and stands facing cross, as if pondering what to do.

At beginning of the second verse, PAST slowly approaches TRAVELER.

At the end of the second verse, the TRAVELER and the PAST join hands and kneel at the cross.

As the final chorus fades, EXIT TRAVELER and PAST holding hands, followed by TIME.

Scene II—The Road Ahead

The Future

STAGE SETTING: Podium, right front. Two chairs center left front, small table beside chair containing copy of script. Cross remains in center back.

ENTER TRAVELER, drags in wearily, chewing bubble gum and carrying a map containing script. Plops down and starts to study the map.

ENTER TIME, looking a little less frazzled than in Scene I.

TIME: So I, Time, march on. Whether you sit or run, I march on at the same pace . . . sixty seconds a minute, sixty minutes an hour, twenty-four hours a day, seven days a week. Months, years, decades, centuries pass.

To the child waiting for Christmas, I drag; to the mother preparing for the holiday, I race. To the grandmother in the nursing home, the years are short—the hours long.

Today becomes yesterday, and tomorrow today.

The past lengthens—the future shortens—and the present is squeezed in a vise between the two.

It's strange how the past that once haunted you can become your friend, your source of wisdom and strength, once you face it at the crossroads of life.

TIME: *(to Traveler)* I see you've slowed down quite a bit since we last visited.

TRAVELER: *(looks up in surprise)* Oh, it's you. You're still around.

TIME: You'd better hope I stay around.

TRAVELER: Yeah . . . well, I do.

TIME: I say, you've slowed down since the last time we visited.

TRAVELER: *(sighs wearily)* Yes, I've just got two gears . . . overdrive and park! *(holds up map)* I didn't realize how tired I was until I stopped running from the past . . . I am exhausted!

TIME: But you can't just park!

TRAVELER: *(angrily)* Says who? I have, haven't I? When I'm in overdrive, you scold me for hurrying. When I park, you don't like that either. I wish you'd quit bugging me.

TIME: Sorry. I didn't mean to bug you . . . but time's wasting and—

TRAVELER: And I've got a long ways to go . . . I know! I know! It's a good thing I traded that scooter in for a Honda Accord. I'd never make it on foot.

TIME: Few people can make it through life on their own power.

TRAVELER: But even with my Honda, I don't know if I can make it. *(holds up map)* Look at the road ahead of me. See this spaghetti bowl? Freeways everywhere! How'll I ever find the right road?
    And what's this? Mountains? Phantom Canyon Road? Where'd the interstates go? Looks like a long one-lane gravel road through the mountains.

ENTER WORRY, wearing a black cape and half mask, sneaks up on TRAVELER.

TRAVELER: (shaking head slowly, studies map) And here's a desert. And what's this? A jungle? I can't believe it. But it sure looks like a jungle. Whew! *(wipes brow)* I don't know . . . I just don't know if I can. . . .

WORRY: *(pounces on Traveler)* BOOO!

TRAVELER: *(drops the map, jumps up, screaming)* YEEEEEKKK! Whatwhat? Whoooooo? Who are you?

WORRY: Oh, you know me. I've lived with you for years. You spend a lot of your time entertaining me.

TRAVELER: *(shudders)* I entertain you? I must be hard up for guests.

WORRY: I'm not a guest. I'm a resident. I'm the last one you see before you go to sleep and I wake you up in the mornings. You even see me in your dreams.

TRAVELER: But who are you and w-w-w-hat are you doing here?

WORRY: *(sneers)* That's a stupid question for you to ask. You brought me!

TRAVELER: I brought you? I certainly did not.

WORRY: Oh, but you did. I've been such a part of your life for so long, I'm second nature to you. If you aren't worrying, you feel guilty.

TRAVELER: Worrying . . . Ohhhh, now, I know who you are. You're that sneaky, sticky creature, Worry.

WORRY: And you are right—although you seldom call me "Worry." Usually, you call me "a burden." And you kneel down with me right beside you as you weep and cry and whine and beg God for mercy. Sometimes you even call me "love." *(mimics)* "Oh, I love them so much, I worry about them all the time."

TRAVELER: I don't think I like you.

WORRY: Oh, I know that, but it doesn't worry me. But you're worried . . . you're worried right now, aren't you?

TRAVELER: No! No, I'm not the least bit worried. I've faced the past. I've been to the cross and I'm not running away anymore. I'm not afraid—not even of you.

WORRY: *(laughs)* So you say! So you say. You've faced the past so you think your troubles are all over. But have you looked at the road ahead? What about the future?

TRAVELER: Of course, I've looked ahead. I'm not worried about the future. I have a map to guide me.

WORRY: Uhhuh . . . and you saw that spaghetti bowl, that tangle of freeways? And you're not worried! Ha! You know you can never make it through that tangled mass of freeways. Why you can't blow a bubble and rub your stomach at the same time.

TRAVELER: I certainly can. I'll show you. *(proceeds to try)*

WORRY: *(mocks)* See I said you couldn't.

TRAVELER: I can too. You're just making me nervous.

WORRY: And that spaghetti bowl doesn't make you nervous?

TRAVELER: Certainly not. I'll just follow the signs.

WORRY: Ha! There's no way you can read the signs fast enough to change lanes to get on the right roads.

TRAVELER: Yes, I can.

WORRY: You cannot.

TRAVELER: I can.

WORRY: Cannot.

TRAVELER: Can too.

WORRY: Can three.

TRAVELER: Can four.

WORRY: For what?

TRAVELER: For . . . for . . . for . . . forgetting those things which are behind, I press forward . . .

WORRY: Yeah, go right ahead, go forward . . . but you're going to get so tangled up in that spaghetti bowl, it'll take a forklift to pull you out.

TRAVELER: *(puts hands over ears)* I'm not going to listen to you, Worry. For years you've been tormenting me. I'm not going to listen to you any more.

WORRY: *(points beyond Traveler, whispers)* And do you know what's over that next hill?

TRAVELER: *(eyes wide stares at Worry, begins shaking)* I can't hear you. I don't want to hear you.

WORRY: *(still pointing and whispering)* Have you ever traveled that road before?

TRAVELER: *(takes hands off ears—in raspy whisper)* What did you say? Why are you whispering?

WORRY: Do you know what's over the next hill? Have you ever traveled that road before?

TRAVELER: No! No! But I've got a map.

WORRY: Ha! Lot of good that will do you! Probably outdated. You could meet the devil head-on at the top of the next hill.

TRAVELER: The d-d-devil? I could m-m-meet the d-d-d-devil? Maybe I could take a d-d-d-detour.

WORRY: Did you know that sixty-five percent of all accidents are caused by drunk drivers? You may never make it home.

TRAVELER: Oh, no! *(grabs for slip strap)* My slip strap is pinned on! Whatever will they think of me in the morgue? I'll be embarrassed to death!

WORRY: Have you ever been on Phantom Canyon Road?

TRAVELER: *(shaking)* No.

WORRY: It's a one-lane gravel road filled with sharp hairpin curves up and down the mountain.

TRAVELER: Hairpin curves?

WORRY: Hairpin curves! Sheer cliffs on one side and dropoffs on the other.

TRAVELER: Cliffs? Dropoffs? Curves? *(grabs stomach)* I get carsick if there are too many curves. And heights make me dizzy.

WORRY: You never know what you'll meet around one of those

curves. A cancer may be waiting to pounce on you. Did you know that one person out of every four has cancer in his or her lifetime?

TRAVELER: Oh, I didn't know that. I had a pain in my big toe last week. Do you think I might have bone cancer?

WORRY: *(shrugs and grins)* One out of four—you could be the one . . . And do you know one and a half marriages out of every two end in divorce?

TRAVELER: One and a half marriages out of two? I think I've got the half one. . . . Divorce?

WORRY: Do you know where your husband is right now?

TRAVELER: Why, he's home . . . home with the kids.

WORRY: You think he's home with the kids, but do you know? Remember last week when he was ten minutes late getting home from work? Where do you think he was then?

TRAVELER: I-I-I th-th-thought he was buying a l-l-loaf of bread. Do you think . . . Ohhhhh, he couldn't be . . . He wouldn't do that to me. . . . Would he?

WORRY: *(shrugs and grins)* Wouldn't he? Better men than he have fallen. And then there's that jungle. What's going to happen to your kids when they go through that jungle? Do you know, sixty percent of all high school kids have experimented with drugs. . . . eighty percent have got drunk at least once. . . . sixty-five percent of all girls have lost their virtue by the time they graduate from high school. . . . ninety-five percent. . . .

TRAVELER: Stop! Stop! I don't want to hear another word. *(collapses into sobs)* Oh, I'm so worried. I'm so afraid. I'm about to have a panic attack! I think I'm going to hyperventilate. Has anybody got a paper sack? Quick get me a paper sack. *(gasping, grabbing for slip strap)* I've got to get that safety pin off. . . . What if I have to go to the hospital?

TIME rushes to her with a paper sack. She works over the Traveler, urging her to "take a deep breath, just relax" while Worry gloats and jumps for glee. Finally things settle back down and Time goes back to podium.

TRAVELER: Oh whatever is going to happen to me? *(buries head in lap, moaning)*

ENTER PAST, dressed in old-fashioned attire. Plays grandmotherly part. WORRY glares at her.

WORRY: And who are you?

PAST: Oh, no, another one of those Israelites.

WORRY: Israelites? I'm not an Israelite.

PAST: Oh, yes, you are. You're a mumbler. Now speak up.

WORRY: *(yells)* I said, who are you?

PAST: I am the Past.

TRAVELER looks up and smiles.

WORRY: Oh, I'm not worried about you. You're on my side. You're her greatest worry. *(frowns and peers closely at Past)* But you look different. What happened to you?

TRAVELER: *(jumps to her feet and runs to hug Past)* Oh, I'm so glad you're here.

WORRY: What? You're glad she's here?

TRAVELER: *(clings to Past)* I'm s-s-soooo worried. I'm terrified.

PAST: About what, my child?

TRAVELER: The future! I don't know what's ahead. It could be anything . . . cancer, divorce, drugs, safety pins. The map shows a spaghetti bowl. . . .

PAST: A spaghetti bowl on a map? You shouldn't use a map for a tablecloth.

TRAVELER: What?

PAST: I said you shouldn't use a map for a tablecloth.

TRAVELER: But I didn't.

PAST: Then how'd spaghetti get on it?

TRAVELER: Spaghetti? Oh, the spaghetti bowl. I guess they didn't have spaghetti bowls in your day.

PAST: Why, we certainly did too. It was one of my favorite dishes.

TRAVELER: But, Granny, it's not spaghetti like you eat. It's a tangled mass of highways. It's just called a "spaghetti bowl." If you don't know where you're going, you can never get there.

PAST: What? Say that again.

TRAVELER: *(louder)* If you don't know where you're going, you can never get there.

PAST: Well, that's the truth . . . always has been. Nothing complicated about that.

WORRY: I want to know what's going on here. *(to Traveler)* How come you are chatting away with the Past like she's your best friend? *(to Past)* And why do you look so different? What's going on here?

TRAVELER: She *is* my friend.

WORRY: She is? Last time I saw you, you were running away from her, scared to death she was going to catch you.

PAST: She stopped and faced me. I'm no longer a ghost that haunts her. She left the guilt and bitterness at the cross. Now she sees me entirely differently. I bring her pleasant, happy, comforting memories.

WORRY: *(to audience)* Well, well, I've heard of people becoming ghosts, but I never heard of a ghost becoming a person.

TRAVELER: *(to Past)* Please, Grannie, help me. I'm so worried.

WORRY: *(aside, to audience)* They can talk about the cross all they want to—she's not out my reach!

TRAVELER: What if I meet the devil head-on at the top of the next hill?

PAST: *(sits down)* Let's sit down. Looks like we need to do a little reminiscing.

BOTH sit down.

PAST: Now, child, remember the time you were in high school and the devil hit you head-on? You just knew your life would be wrecked if you didn't go his way—you wouldn't have any friends—you'd lose that college scholarship. Remember?

As the TRAVELER and the PAST reminisce, WORRY rejoices or frets, depending upon what is being said. She doesn't say anything, simply makes motions to convey her feelings. Every time something positive is said, WORRY fades farther into the background until she EXITS.

TRAVELER: Yes, I remember.

PAST: What happened?

TRAVELER: Well, I submitted my will to God. I decided I was going to do right if no one else in the whole school did.

PAST: And?

TRAVELER: When I took a stand for right, half the faculty and lots of the kids backed me. They even changed the school policy.

PAST: And?

TRAVELER: By the time it was over I had more friends than I'd ever had, and I got two scholarships.

PAST: You resisted the devil and he fled. So what happens if you meet the devil head-on? You submit to God and resist the devil. You sent the devil packing once; you can do it again.

TRAVELER: I guess I can. But . . . but look at this map. See this Phantom Canyon Road?

PAST: Can I hoe? Honey, I reckon I can. I always had the biggest garden in the county.

TRAVELER: I said see this Phantom Canyon Road? It's a one-lane road with two-way traffic. There are hairpins curves and cliffs and dropoffs. Why, you never know what you're going to meet around the next curve.

PAST: That's true. You never know. The Good Book says, *Boast not thyself of to morrow; for thou knowest not what a day may bring forth* (Proverbs 27:1).

TRAVELER: Ooooooohhhh, anything could happen tomorrow; the Bible says so. I'm so worried that *(husband)* is going to get tired of me and . . .

PAST: Whoa! Stop right there! Let's go back to Phantom Canyon Road. I've been there. You never know what's around the next curve. . . . It could be a canyon filled with pretty flowers and a crystal stream just a sparklin' . . . a mountain peak kissed by fluffy clouds . . . a deer grazing on a patch of green carpet.

TRAVELER: But it could be danger . . . or death . . . or the d-d-devil.

PAST: But it could just as easily be beauty and life.

TRAVELER: I hadn't thought of that. . . . I guess . . . I guess it could be . . . beauty and life.

PAST: Tomorrow could bring blessings beyond your wildest dreams, honey. Remember the time you were scared to death your church was going to fall away to nothing and instead the Lord gave you a great revival?

TRAVELER: Oh, yes, I remember.

PAST: Remember the time you thought you had cancer of the stomach, but you'd just been eating too much fried food and needed to go on a diet?

TRAVELER: That's almost as bad as cancer. . . . No. No, I don't mean that. But what about that jungle my kids are going to have to go through . . . drugs, liquor, immorality? I'm worried sick about them.

PAST: *Jesus Christ, the same yesterday, to day and for ever.* He kept you in high school. He'll keep your children in high school.

TRAVELER: But it's different now. . . . Times have changed.

PAST: Changed? Yes and no. There have always been temptations . . . and there has always been an escape route for those who looked for it.

TRAVELER: *(stands up and helps Past to her feet)* Oh, Granny, you're such a comfort to me. It's hard to believe I once ran from you. With you beside me, I don't have to worry about the future.

PAST: Yep, like I always say: "It came to pass. . . ."

EXIT as song begins.

SONG: "I Don't Know About Tomorrow"

Scene III: EnJOYing the Trip

The Present

STAGE SETTING: Same as in Scene II.

SONG: "We Have This Moment Today"

During second chorus TIME ENTERS, goes to podium. Recitation to be given between the second chorus and third verse. Music plays softly in the background.

TIME: Moments—that's what time is made of.
 That's what life is made of—moments. That's what memories are made of.
 And that's all of Time you have—this moment.
 Look. In your hand you hold the precious present.
 Is the present lost to you as you mourn over the past and fear the future?
 Stop! Gather this moment close to your bosom. Feel it! *(pause)* Sense it! *(pause)*
 You sit in the presence of the King and His daughters. Are you alive? Are you awake? Are you aware of His presence? Do you realize the value of the precious present?
 You have only the present—this moment, today.

SONG: "We Have This Moment, Today" *(last verse and chorus)*

TIME: Some people run ahead of me and others lag behind. A few, a very few, are content to walk beside me.

Some sit and fret. Others hurry and worry. A few, a very few, enjoy the trip.

Some live in "the good old days." Others live for "someday." Some . . .

ENTER TRAVELER, from back, stumbling and staggering, moaning and groaning. She stops every little bit to search and asks weakly: "I'm so weak I don't know if I can go another step. But I've got to find her. Have you seen her? I can't believe I lost her again. Are you sure she's not hiding behind you? I can't go on without her."

TIME: And what's the matter with you, friend traveler? The last time I saw you you had faced the Past and defeated Worry. You were ready to travel on.

TRAVELER: I am a poor, wayfaring traveler, so weak and weary. Do you reckon a vitamin B-12 shot would help me?

TIME: I'm afraid you need more than vitamins. Sometimes I think you're hopeless.

TRAVELER: Not hopeless, Joy-less. Have you seen her?

TIME: Her? Who is "her?"

TRAVELER: Joy. I've lost my Joy. Have you seen her?

TIME: Have I seen her? Look around you. There are some *(number)* women here and you ask me if I've seen Joy. For all I know there may be sixteen Joys here. What's her full name?

TRAVELER: N. Joy.

TIME: N. Joy? Hummmm . . . that name sounds familiar. What does she look like?

TRAVELER: Look like? Well, to be honest, I've forgotten. But I've got to find her. I'm getting weaker by the moment. *(wails)* If I don't find her, I'll die . . . I just know I will.

TIME: You've forgotten what she looks like? Then how will you know her if you find her?

TRAVELER: That's a good question.

TIME: How long have you been looking for her?

TRAVELER: A looooooong time. I can't decide if she is ahead of me or behind me. Can I sit down here? I'm too weak to stand.

TIME: Here, let me help you. *(gets her settled in a chair)* Now when was the last time you saw her?

TRAVELER: Uhhhhhh, the last time I saw her was . . . Christmas? No, come to think of it I didn't even see her then. I was so stressed out . . . Couldn't you give us a little extra time at Christmas? There's so much to do. . . .

TIME: You're celebrating Christmas from Halloween to New Year's now. If you had more time, you'd just plan more activities. But back to Joy . . . when was the last time you saw her?

TRAVELER: When I graduated? Noooo, I was too worried about getting a job. You know that old sneak Worry has robbed me of a lot of time I could have spent with Joy! Makes me so mad just to think about it! *(jumps to her feet—stands the rest of the time)*

ENTER THE PAST, dressed as in Scene II.

TRAVELER: Oh, here's Granny now. Maybe she can help me.

PAST: Help you what, child?

TRAVELER: Help me find Joy. I've got to find her; she's my strength. If I don't find her, I just know I'll die. *(looks horror struck)* Oooooh, do you suppose she's dead? *(wails loudly)* What if I never see her again until the journey's end? You know, like the old song says: *(sings sorrowfully)*
"On the streets of glory, let me lift my voice,
Cares all past, home at last, ever to rejoice."

PAST: *(aside to audience)* I heard that! *(to Traveler)* You're forgetting the first part of that song. *(sings)* "As I journey through the land singing as I go . . ."

TRAVELER: Singing? You don't expect me to sing when my Joy's gone, do you? If you just knew what I've been going through. *(wails)* The garage door opener's locked up. The riding lawn mower's broken down, and the water bed has a leak in it!

PAST: The water bed has a leak in it? My lands, in my day, child, we put water in buckets. *(sarcastically)* You sure are having it rough!

TRAVELER: And that's not the half of it. My son's teacher said he was immature.

PAST: And what grade is he in?

TRAVELER: Kindergarten! And all of the boys in my daughter's Sunday school class make fun of her. All of them! And in Sunday school, too!

PAST: Why, I declare I don't know what this generation's comin' to . . . kids makin' fun of kids. Now that's somethin' new! And how old is she?

TRAVELER: Eight. And now my Joy has died. I just know she has. I'll never see her again until the end of the road. *(wails and carries on)*

PAST: Let me assure you, child, that Joy's not dead.

TRAVELER: You've seen her?

PAST: Yes, but not in your presence—at least, not lately.

TRAVELER: Oh, Granny, help me find her. If I could just remember when I last saw her. I don't know if she's ahead of me or behind me.

PAST: It's always the past or the future, isn't it, child? What about the present . . . right here . . . right now?

TRAVELER: Oh, I know she's not right here, right now. I've looked. Of course, I can't remember what she looks like . . . soooo I may have overlooked her.

PAST: Now think, child. Use your noodle. If you can't remember when you last saw her, maybe you can remember where. Where were you the last time you saw Joy?

TRAVELER: Hummmmm . . . where was I the last time I saw Joy? At the fair? No, some silly kid got cotton candy in my hair. Took a week to get it all washed out. At the mall? No . . . the very same dress I bought last week at half price was seventy-five percent off this week. Happens to me every time. Makes me so mad! Now where was I the last time I saw Joy? Hummmmm . . . oh, now I remember, *(slowly and emphatically)* I was in the presence of the King. *(pause)* Come to think of it, that's where I usually find Joy . . . in the presence of the King. I wonder how we got separated.

PAST: You got caught up in the rat race of life and—

TRAVELER: But, Granny, I've got to run this race. Don't you remember . . . Paul said to run the race. I've got to beat the clock!

PAST: Feed the flock? Child, that's the preacher's job.

TRAVELER: I said I've got to run this race. I've got to beat the clock!

SOUND: TICKING OF CLOCK

PAST: Child, life is not a fifty-yard dash. It's an endurance race.

TRAVELER: An endurance race? Like, *[She] that endureth to the end, the same shall be saved?*

PAST: Yes, like that. You got caught up in the wrong race—the rat race. Let me ask you a question. How long has it been since you made time to sit in the presence of the King? That's where you'll find the fullness of Joy.

TRAVELER: Well . . . well . . . *(looks around in amazement—stands slowly)* Why, that's where I am right now . . . right here! Right now! I'm in the presence of the King—with His daughters. And I almost missed this moment . . . I almost let it slip through my fingers. *(slowly straightens as if strength is flowing through her)* And look, Granny, I see Joy. I see her. I see Joy reflected in the faces of these lovely, godly women who are sitting in the presence of the King. I've found Joy!

PAST: The joy you see radiating on the faces of these ladies is the beauty of holiness, child. May we never lose it.

TRAVELER: Amen! And may I never again lose my Joy. Now I have strength for the journey. I can enJOY the trip.

TRAVELER skips from the stage followed by PAST.

SONG: Medley of joyful choruses by congregation

Index

AUDIENCE PARTICIPATION
    Creating a Centerpiece – *33*
    Getting Acquainted – *34*
    Giving Roses Now – *12*
    Just Imagine – *76*
    Let's Make Music – *64*
    Mirror Images—Sign In – *67*
    Mothers Memorial Is . . . – *49*
    My Mother Said – *42*
    Piece Work – *82*
    The Story of My Bible – *19*
    Who Am I? (The Revealing) – *19*

CONTESTS
    A Flower Show – *11*
    A Quilt Booth – *81*
    Creating a Centerpiece – *33*

DRAMA
    A Goodly Heritage – *99*
    A Role Play – *131*
    And There Was Music (musical monologue) – *64*
    Hand-Me-Down Faith (monologue) – *34*
    My Memory's Fine (monologue) – *83*
    School Days – *159*
    The Race – *183*
    The Senior Saints' Quilting Bee (pantomime) – *85*

GAMES
    An Ear for Music – *63*
    Fairy Tales – *76*
    Mirror Images: The A-mazing Mirror – *68*
    Mothers Memorial Is . . . – *49*
    Piece Work – *82*
    Simon Looks in the Mirror – *69*
    Wash It – *89*
    Who Am I? (The Revealing) – *19*

IDEAS FOR SPEAKERS
    Christ's Reflection – *73*
    Contend for the Faith – *38*
    Our Wonder-Full World – *80*
    Pieced Together – *86*

PROGRAM SPECIALS
    And There Was Music – *64*
    Mothers in Israel – *43*

PUZZLES
    A Soap Opera – *87*
    Acronyms – *47*
    Image Makers – *69*
    Kinds of Women (crossword) – *18*
    Riddles – *63*
    Say It with Flowers – *11*
    Take Note – *61*
    Thinker-Toys – *75*

QUIZZES
    A Quilter's Quiz – *81*
    Bath Time – *88*
    Three-Generation Bible Families – *34*
    Whose Mother Said? – *41*

SKITS
    A Mother-Daughter Tea – *26*
    Annie Body – *76*
    Fretful Flowers – *13*
    Hanging out the Wash – *89*
    In Whose Image? – *70*
    Mrs. Skinflint's Surgery – *56*
    Nothing New under the Sun – *20*
    The First Ladies Auxiliary Project – *49*